NO
half-truths
ALLOWED
STUDY GUIDE

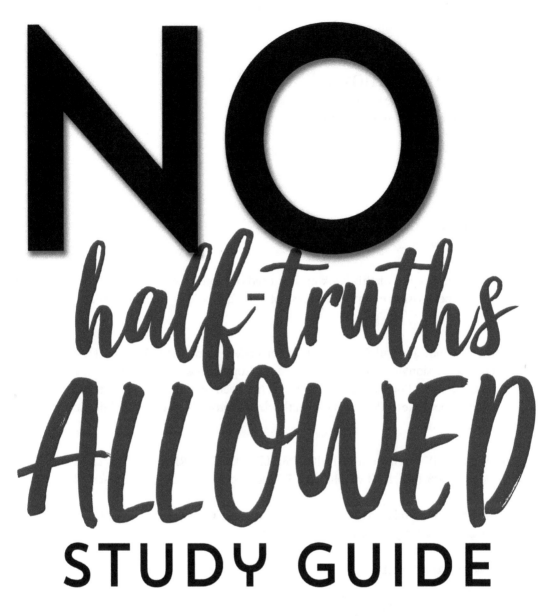

NO
half-truths
ALLOWED
STUDY GUIDE

Understanding the Complete Gospel Message

CHRISTINE PAXSON & ROSE SPILLER

Ambassador International
GREENVILLE, SOUTH CAROLINA & BELFAST, NORTHERN IRELAND

www.ambassador-international.com

No Half-Truths Allowed Study Guide

Understanding the Complete Gospel Message
©2020 by Christine Paxson and Rose Spiller
All rights reserved

ISBN: 978-1-62020-961-5
eISBN: 978-1-62020-987-5

Cover Design and Typesetting by Hannah Nichols
eBook Conversion by Anna Riebe Raats

AMBASSADOR INTERNATIONAL
Emerald House
411 University Ridge, Suite B14
Greenville, SC 29601, USA
www.ambassador-international.com

AMBASSADOR BOOKS
The Mount
2 Woodstock Link
Belfast, BT6 8DD, Northern Ireland, UK
www.ambassadormedia.co.uk

The colophon is a trademark of Ambassador, a Christian publishing company.

CONTENTS

INTRODUCTION

For many Christians, the Gospel message has become commonplace in our thoughts and minds. It's something we hear about so often and talk about so often that we can take it for granted that we have a complete understanding of it. We may convince ourselves that we could explain it or present it at any given time. We trust that our knowledge of it is correct, and that we fully understand what the complete Gospel message is.

But what if you were wrong? What if you found out that the Gospel message you'd been believing and/or presenting was incorrect or had essential parts missing? What if you found out that the gospel message you have been taught and that you were putting your trust in wasn't really the Gospel message at all—or at least not the complete message? What if your understanding of the Gospel was only a half-truth?

Sadly, evangelical churches are filled with people (and pastors) who do not understand the complete Gospel message and who are believing and presenting a gospel message that is incomplete and, in some cases, untrue.

The Gospel is the most important message there is. It's the one message that every human being needs to hear, the only message that can save us, and the most important message for Christians to proclaim to others. Because it's the most important, it's the most important one to get right!

This is exactly why we felt led to write our book, *No Half-Truths Allowed: Understanding the Complete Gospel Message*. This study guide is designed to be a companion to that book. While this study guide can stand alone without the book, it is designed as a supplement to give you a richer and deeper understanding of the Gospel message. For the optimal experience, we suggest going through it with a group. Learning is enriched and more fun when we do it together!

Our hope is that you already have a good understanding of the Gospel message and that this study will enhance what you already know. But if not, we hope that this study helps you to understand your own salvation and present the complete Gospel message to others.

LAYING THE GROUNDWORK

GETTING YOUR TOES WET

What was the last major project you completed?

finishing house after flood / pikler

What did you do to prepare?

just began / plans + research

How did it turn out?

Not finished / great

We would probably all agree that any quality project requires careful planning and skill. This is true whether you are making a quilt, building a deck, or refinishing a rocking chair. Any project we take on that we desire to have a favorable outcome requires a "blueprint" of sorts. This blueprint includes a plan for the finished project, the correct tools, and the skill to make the vision come to life. The same can be said for articulating the Gospel message.

When it comes to understanding the complete Gospel message, what are the:

Plans?

Read the gospels, follow a study guide

Tools?

This book & Bible

Skills?

Prior knowledge & experience

Ask yourself these questions:

Can you articulate the Gospel message on a moment's notice?

Can you adapt your witness to different audiences without changing the message?

Are you prepared for the questions that will inevitably come when you share the Gospel?

Pretty much , yes , not always

If you answered "no" to any of the questions above, what "plans, tools, or skills" are you lacking?

experience w/ testimony & reading, knowing verses - confidence

If you answered "yes" to any of the question above, what "plans, tools, or skills" are you strong in?

Had experience w/ ppl of different levels of faith

Let's begin our journey with what we know and where we are right now. How would you explain to someone what the Gospel is? Below, write down what you would say to a new or non-Christian. This is not meant to be shared. It is just meant for your eyes only, so you can see where you are right now. Then, at the end of this study, we will do this again, so you can compare.

I would say - this world isn't the end for me, as I have been promised another life. If you search you will find.

DIVING IN DEEP

Where do we look to find the full and true Gospel message? It may seem obvious to most of us that the place we should look is the Bible. Our reformer fathers understood this and correctly took the stand that the Bible is to be the only authority on the things of God. It was one of the five tenants that came out of the Reformation. They called it *Sola Scriptura*, which is Latin for "only Scripture." Here are some of the verses they used as proof of *Sola Scriptura*: *How do each of these verses support* Sola Scriptura?

Proverbs 30:5-6

The scripture is the only way. The words of God are perfect, do not add or subtract from His words.

Isaiah 40:8

The word is forever, long after the grass dies.

Matthew 4:4

God's word is main need, cannot live on water alone

Luke 16:17

God or His law never changes

1 Thessalonians 2:13

The Word is not from human's but from God + when you hear it you know.

2 Timothy 3:15-17

You know the scripture since birth – it is all useful in teaching.

These verses, and others, make it very clear that Scripture is the only authority to be used for the things of God—including the Gospel message. Sadly, though, as discussed in *No Half-Truths*, some Christians do not just use the Bible as their only authority. They add in other factors like church tradition, their own experiences, and their own feelings.

Turn to **Mark 7:5-13**. *What does this passage say about using church tradition as an authority?*

the traditions are not God's word

Maybe you didn't know that the Catholic Church uses church tradition as much as, if not more than, the Bible as their authority. Based on Mark 7:5-13, what would your argument against it be?

They are living a lie - against God's words.

Now, let's look at some verses of Scripture that direct us on using experience and emotions as an authority on the things of God. What do these verses show us about the danger of using our feelings and experiences?

Proverbs 14:12

appears to be right = death

Proverbs 19:2-3

Don't jump in w/o knowledge

Proverbs 28:26

don't trust in yourself, trust in God's wisdom.

Jeremiah 17:9

your heart is deceitful

1 Corinthians 1:10-17

don't follow ppl, follow God

Galatians 5:19-21

Acts of flesh will not inherit the kingdom.

There is a place for our feelings and experiences. They are part of the make-up of who we are and will certainly be a part of our testimony of what God has done in our lives. However, they are not to replace the Gospel, and they need to be lined up with Scripture to ensure that they are from God.

What are the essential elements of your personal testimony? The things that you would definitely want to share with someone when witnessing to them?

w/o God my life is empty - no purpose

Have you thought about making sure your testimony lines up with Scripture? Do you think it does? Why is that so crucial?

It is crucial to make sure we are not offline w/ God's commandments and he accepts us into the kingdom

Where Do We Find the Gospel Message in Scripture?

No Half-Truths Allowed says the Gospel, in its simplest form, can be summed up as *God Creates–Man Sins–Christ Redeems–Man Responds*. Let's look at these verses in the Book of Romans. How does each specifically illustrate the prescribed element.

God Creates: Romans 4:17

God gives life to the dead

Man Sins: Romans 1:18-21, Romans 3:11-18

God has made sin clear + they have turned their backs on Him.

Christ Redeems: Romans 3:21-26, 5:6-8

God saves those who come to Him. Christ died for us while we were sinners.

Man Responds: Romans 6:13-22, Romans 12:1-3

Sin shall not be your master, you are under God's grace.

BACK ON DRY LAND

What is the danger of cliché's like, "God loves you," or "You need to find Jesus?"

you have to turn away from sin - not just know
God loves you. - Finding him + accepting him
as Savior are not the same.

Paul used different methods of witnessing depending on his audience, but his Gospel message never changed. *What are some of the different types of audiences you may find yourself witnessing to?*

New believers, ppl that don't understand why I
am a devoted Christian, those who occasionally
go to church but don't lead a Godly life

What are some alterations you can see that you would have to make in your delivery for each of these audiences?

Stop cussing!

SUMMARY

While the Gospel message may be a simple one, there are many complex facets in it. The more we delve into all of those facets and gain an understanding of the theology and doctrine behind them, the clearer and simpler we will be able to articulate the message to others. Why go to all of this work? First, God tells us to. One of the last things Jesus said to His disciples while on Earth was, *"Go into all the world and proclaim the gospel to the whole creation"* (Mark 16:15).

Second, as we said, the Gospel message is the central message of the entire Bible! It is the life-saving, life-transforming message of God! And while God does not need us to save anybody, He gives us the privilege of being part of the process. We have no way of knowing whose heart the Holy Spirit may be regenerating at this very moment! Therefore, we need to witness to as many and as often as we can. We owe it to the person we are witnessing to and to God to present an accurate and complete Gospel message. The Gospel is offensive and humbling. Even with a regenerated heart that gives a person the desire to seek God out, they will have the stumbling block of Jesus Christ, which can include coming to the recognition that we have absolutely nothing of our own to offer God, realizing there is no possible way we could ever save ourselves and need Jesus to do it for us, and understanding that Jesus calls us to live in a sometimes radically different way than the rest of the world. Let us not make our taking away or adding to the message another one!

NOTES

What you win them out, you will win them to →

Book of Romans   God creates
                     Man Sins
                     Christ Redeems } Cycle
                     Man Responds

GOD THE ALMIGHTY CREATOR

GETTING YOUR TOES WET

How much of an emphasis does your church and the Bible studies you have participated in put on learning doctrine and theology?

_____

_____

Do you think it is important that we know and understand the foundations of what we believe? Why or why not?

_____

_____

There are many Christians (and pastors) who hear the words "doctrine" and "theology" and check out. These are words and concepts for old, bearded, biblical scholars, not hip, young Christians! Sadly, this attitude of ignoring doctrine and theology has led to a crisis in our churches—millions of Christians, who are unsure of what they believe, are vulnerable to false teaching and heresy. Tragically, there is a culture within some churches that just want their congregants to be "dumb and in love with Jesus." Friends, we cannot settle for this! We owe it to ourselves, each other, and most importantly, God, to be educated in His Word. In this lesson, we will begin to expand our foundational knowledge of God the Almighty Father.

DIVING IN DEEP

Our Triune God

Before we hone in on God the Father, we should have a basic understanding of the Trinity. The three major truths of the doctrine of the Trinity are:

1.   The Father, Son, and Holy Spirit are distinct Persons;

2.   Each Person is fully God;

3.   There is only one God.

How would you articulate in your own words the doctrine of the Trinity to a new believer?

_____

_____

All Three are God. They are all equal, omnipotent, omniscient, and omnipresent. They are all Three one God, yet three distinct Persons; and All have existed for all time simultaneously. They do, however, each have unique functions. Look up the below verses. *How do they define the distinct role(s) of God the Father, Jesus the Son, and the Holy Spirit?*

Titus 2:13-14

_____

_____

John 14:16-17

_____

_____

Isaiah 64:8

_____

_____

Luke 10:21

_____

_____

John 1:14

_____

_____

Titus 3:5-6

_____

_____

How does having a foundational understanding of God the Father, the Almighty Creator help our understanding of the Gospel and relaying its message to others?

_____

_____

Remember, though, while the Father is never the Son, the Son is never the Holy Spirit, and the Holy Spirit is never the Father, any attribute Scripture ascribes to One of the Persons of the Trinity can also be ascribed to the Other Two.

God the Almighty Father

Jesus, Himself, tells us to refer to His Father as our Father. He even says our prayers should begin with "Our Father in heaven" (Matt. 6:9). By doing this, Jesus is placing God the Father above all else. He is holy and perfect and far above us. The very definition of "holy" means "exalted or worthy of complete devotion as one perfect in goodness and righteousness; consecrated; sacred."[1]

Isaiah 6:3 says it best: *"Holy, holy, holy is the LORD of hosts; the whole earth is full of his glory."* God's holiness is not just one of His attributes like wisdom, justice, or love; it permeates everything He does, says, or thinks. It is in every fiber of His being; It is Who He is!

How do these verses further exemplify the holiness of God?

Exodus 15:11

_____

_____

1 Samuel 2:2

_____

_____

Psalm 99:5

_____

_____

Revelation 4:8

_____

_____

---

1   Merriam-Webster, s.v. "Holy," accessed April 07, 2019, https://www.merriam-webster.com/dictionary/holy.

Hopefully, we have a grasp on what the biblical authors understood. God is perfect and so much higher than us that He is beyond our full comprehension. He is deserving of our praise, worship, and complete devotion. He is holy!

God the Almighty Creator

The first part of our simplified Gospel message is "God creates." We need only to open our Bibles to the very first verse to have this confirmed. **Genesis 1:1** says, "In the beginning, God created the heavens and the earth." This is the very essence of Who God the Father is.

Romans 1:20 tells us that creation shows us the attributes of God the Creator.

In what ways do you see creation revealing the attributes of God the Creator?

_____

_____

Think back to Lesson 1 when we talked about the importance of having a finished "blueprint" for any project for which we expect a favorable outcome. God had a finished plan for the entire world before He ever created it. From the point of Creation until the time Jesus comes back, every human who ever lived is part of that plan. Both believers and non-believers!

Have you ever thought about non-believers being part of God's plan?

_____

_____

Let's look at some verses that illustrate this. *How is God's sovereign plan being furthered in the following verses?*

Exodus 3:21-22, 4:21

_____

_____

1 Samuel 15:2-3

_____

_____

Mark 4:11-12

_____

_____

Romans 9:11-13

_____

_____

Some of these verses are hard to read and even harder to understand. We are in the midst of God's plan and can't always grasp the purpose behind what He is doing. That is where faith comes in. We have to trust that God, Who is completely sovereign, is also completely good and completely just and knows exactly what He is doing. *Everyone* has been created for a purpose and has a place in God's plan. While the ultimate purpose of all men is to glorify God and enjoy Him forever, God has created each of us with a specific, tailor-made purpose that is just for us!

Does knowing you have a specific part to play in God's plan for the world give you confidence or anxiety? Why?

_____

_____

_____

We need never fear we are outside of the decretive will of God. The decretive will of God is that which is unseen, and usually unknown, to us. Who was, is, and will be saved is an example of this. We have no way of knowing this. It is at God's pleasure whom He has chosen to be saved. Another example is when Jesus will return to Earth. God has revealed that He, indeed, will return, but it is not for us to know the exact time.

We are not to concern ourselves with God's decretive will. In fact, trying to discern it can put us in the precarious situation of presuming we can read the mind of God. Instead, we are to concentrate on God's preceptive will. God's preceptive will is the will of God that is revealed to us in Scripture. It is how God expects us, as His children, to purport ourselves. This is the will we should strive to learn by studying Scripture. This is also the will we sin against by disobeying the precepts and principles God has laid out for us. Since we are created by God, we are owned by God. He has the right to tell us how He wants us to live.

Take a look at **Romans 9:19-21**. *How does this verse illustrate the point that we are created and owned by God, and therefore, He can direct us to how we are to live?*

_____

_____

_____

BACK ON DRY LAND

Justice Brings Forth Punishment

If everything about God is holy, then it stands to reason that His justice is also holy. What is holy justice?

_____

_____

What does "everyone getting what they deserve" look like to you?

_____

_____

This is always the part of God that people will balk at. How could a perfectly loving God punish people for messing up? While God is certainly perfect Love, it does not cancel out His perfect justice; in fact, it enhances it! Would God's love be perfect if He ignored sin? No, it wouldn't. It would make Him inconsistent, untrustworthy, immoral, and, worst of all, weak.

Can you think of an example of how God overlooking sin would negate His perfect love?

_____

_____

How would you explain this concept to a new or non-believer when they say, "How can a loving God send people to Hell?"

_____

_____

SUMMARY

Just as good cannot exist without evil, happiness cannot exist without sadness, and joy cannot exist without pain, neither can the saving work of Jesus exist without the punishment we need saving from! Only when we understand the holiness of God the Almighty Creator and Father can we understand the seriousness of our sin against that holy God. That comprehension makes the saving work of Jesus all the sweeter.

Having a healthy reverence for God and His magnificence is the biblical definition of the "fear of God." As our favorite verse Proverbs 9:10 says, "The fear of the Lord is the beginning of wisdom, and the knowledge of the Holy One is insight."

NOTES

DEAD AS A DOOR NAIL

GETTING YOUR TOES WET

What is humanity's purpose? Do you know your purpose?

_____

_____

Do you think of yourself as a "pretty good" person?

_____

_____

How do you think God feels about you?

_____

_____

If someone told you that you need rescuing from God's wrath and punishment when you die, would you believe them?

_____

_____

Most people, at some point in their life, have at least some basic, fundamental questions about God, the Bible, or what's going to happen to them when they die. For anyone who's grown up in America (and probably elsewhere, too), it's likely that you have some ideas planted in your head by Sunday school teachers, parents, and maybe even from television commercials of Heaven, Hell, sin, the devil, and angels. In the space below, *write down some thoughts you have about some or all of these things. It doesn't have to be detailed; just write down what you know (or at least think you know) about them.*

_____

_____

Ask yourself these questions:

What does God think about me when I do something "bad"?

_____

_____

What does God think about me when I do something "good"?

_____

_____

What is sin?

_____

_____

Do you believe people are born innocent?

_____

_____

Why do people do bad things? Did someone have to teach them to be "bad"?

_____

_____

_____

When someone treats you or someone you love unjustly, or you see injustices and atrocities in the world today, what do you want to see happen to those responsible for the pain and suffering?

_____

_____

_____

Do you want justice for yourself/others, or do you want the perpetrator to be overlooked and let go freely, without any consequences at all?

_____

_____

_____

As we dive into the next part, keep your answers to these questions in mind.

DIVING IN DEEP

Why Did God Create Us?

One of the most fundamental questions all humans have is "What is my purpose?" To understand why we were created, we need to know Who created us in the first place. Look up the following verses to find the answers to these two questions:

Who created us?

Genesis 1:26-27; Psalm 139:13; Isaiah 45:12; Revelation 4:11

_____

_____

What is our purpose according to each verse?

Psalm 50:15

_____

_____

Isaiah 43:7

_____

_____

Matthew 5:16

_____

_____

John 17:5

_____

_____

Romans 15:6

_____

_____

Colossians 1:16

_____

_____

Why did we list so many verses to answer the last two questions? Because it is *imperative* that we understand why we were created! The verses that answer the last two questions show us that we were created **by God** and that He created us **to glorify Him**. We were created to show just how glorious God is. We are to reflect His glory, to be like Him, and to do the good works He planned in advance for us to do. And by us doing those things, **He will be glorified**. If this turns things upside down a bit for you, that's no surprise because you're probably used to hearing that God's focus and desire is to see His *creatures* glorified! This is what much of the evangelical Christian world is focused on teaching today. We have made what God is doing about *us*. It is not. God is out for His own glory, not for ours.

A Fall in the Garden

What went wrong in the world God had created? Why do people do bad things? *Read* **Genesis 2:15** *and* **Genesis 3:1-7**. This is what is referred to by Christians as "the fall of man," the moment humanity sinned against God. This was not just about some fruit. This was the parents of the whole human race deciding and declaring that they did not want to be ruled by God! Instead, they wanted to make their own decisions. This was Adam and Eve rejecting their Creator!

What were the consequences of this sin?

Genesis 2:17

_____

_____

Genesis 3:14-19

_____

_____

How did this affect all the rest of humanity from that time on?

Romans 5:12-21

_____

_____

1 Corinthians 15:21-22

_____

_____

Our first parents were created with the ability to not sin. But they did. And at the fall, Adam and Eve's sin infected all of humanity from that time on. Every single person is born with a sin nature that is hostile to God. We are not born innocent, nor are we basically good, as the world teaches. We are sinful from birth and are born enemies of God.

What do the following verses say about humans?

Genesis 8:21

_____

_____

Job 15:14-16

_____

_____

Psalm 51:5

_____

_____

Psalm 58:3

_____

_____

Isaiah 59:2

_____

_____

Romans 5:10

_____

_____

Romans 8:5-11

_____

_____

Colossians 1:21-22

_____

_____

Often, we think of sin as individual, isolated things we do that are "bad." We think of sin as "messing up" or "making mistakes," but not as something that offends God, Who is perfectly holy! Sin is not forgetting to meet your friend for lunch. Sin is the disobedience of God's Law, and disobedience to it is not something that should be referred to as mess-ups or mistakes! It is so important, in fact, that blood had to be shed for even our unintentional sin!

God is not only perfectly holy, but He is also perfectly just! If we are robbed, we want our stuff back, or at the very least, restitution from the thief! When we see children hurt by an adult, we want the adult in jail! When we see cruelty to animals, we want justice done for what the poor creatures suffered. Everyone resonates with the idea of justice. That should be no surprise because our Creator is just. And because He is, He cannot overlook our sin. Did you get that? Our *perfectly holy and perfectly just* God demands justice for our sin! And yes, even for the things we so much want to claim are "mistakes" and "mess-ups." Ouch!

DEAD AS A DOOR NAIL

Our indwelling sin nature has left us in a very bad predicament—we are dead in it. Just like a cadaver lying on an autopsy table, we're dead. And dead men cannot move their arms or legs, or open their eyes, or think, or do anything. We are the same when it comes to making ourselves right with God. We have no way of trying to not be His enemy. We have no way of offering justice for what we've done. We can do *absolutely nothing* to save ourselves. Dead men can't reach out for God. Dead men can't go searching for God. Dead men wouldn't even be able to think of doing such things. This is where we find ourselves. Note what each of the following verses says about us:

Psalm 14:2-3

_____

_____

Psalm 53:2-3

_____

_____

Isaiah 65:1

_____

_____

Jeremiah 4:22

_____

_____

Romans 3:10-18

_____

_____

Colossians 2:13

_____

_____

Ephesians 2:1-3

_____

_____

We are born separated from our Creator and deserving of His wrath. Hell is real. And every single human being deserves to be there for eternity because there is no one without sin. God doesn't base His judgement of who deserves hell on how good we are compared to our fellow human beings. We're all born with a sin nature. We are born sinners, hostile to God, and with no inclination to seek Him. We're all deserving of His wrath. We may even sit in church with people who will suffer God's wrath. What does Jude's warning about false teachers say about it in **Jude 1:4-19**?

_____

_____

Regardless of what some people claim, or what we may want to believe, there are warnings about Hell in the Bible. What do these verses tell us about Hell?

Matthew 8:12

_____

_____

Matthew 24:50-51

_____

_____

Matthew 25:30, 41-46

_____

_____

Luke 16:22-28

_____

_____

Revelation 20:11-15

_____

_____

BACK ON DRY LAND

What is the danger in not realizing that we've offended our perfectly holy, perfectly just God, even with the sins we consider "little"?

_____

_____

Since the thrust of this book is not only making sure we understand the complete Gospel message ourselves but also making sure that others understand it, too, can you think of some ways you've heard sin talked about in the past that didn't give the whole picture and that made sin seem less important than it is?

_____

_____

Has this lesson changed how you think about your relationship with God? If so, how?

_____

_____

SUMMARY

If this lesson seemed like a downer, it was supposed to! It's important to understand that you and I were effectively "dead as a door nail" with no inclination to seek God, no desire to seek Him, and actually as an enemy of His, deserving of His wrath. Only by knowing that can a non-Christian understand the dire position they are in. This is the only way they will see their need for a Savior. And only by knowing that can a Christian fully appreciate what Jesus, the Savior, has done for them! Hang on! The good news is coming!

NOTES

_____

_____

_____

_____

_____

_____

_____

_____

_____

_____

_____

_____

_____

_____

_____

_____

_____

_____

_____

_____

_____

_____

_____

_____

BOUND TO SIN, THEN FREED TO LIVE RIGHTEOUSLY

GETTING YOUR TOES WET

What things have you heard preachers claim will happen for you if you become a Christian?

_____

_____

What reasons do preachers and pastors give for coming forth at an altar call?

_____

_____

Do you ever find yourself trying to please God by being good, only to get discouraged because you find yourself back in the same cycle of sin you were striving to be free from?

_____

_____

If you are a Christian, do you experience the freedom we have in Christ? Or do you wonder what "freedom(s)" the songs we sing are talking about?

_____

_____

Bound to Sin

Like we learned in the last lesson, Adam and Eve's fall left us with a sin nature that is hostile to God. Like a man with a ball and chain hooked to him, we are *bound* to our sin. And it can get to be quite a heavy burden. We are totally depraved, meaning there isn't one part of us that is untouched by sin. That doesn't mean we are as bad as we could possibly be. But it does mean that everything we do is tainted with sin to the point that even our "good deeds" are like filthy rags. Why are the good deeds of a non-Christian "like filthy rags" to God (Isa. 64:6 NIV)? Because they are not done for His glory.

Like we said before, everyone has an inborn sin nature, and we are all like dead men—we need a heart jumpstart! Just like a dead man can't reach out for the paddles, and a car with a dead battery can't hook itself up to jumper cables, we need God to regenerate our cold, dead, stony hearts because we are incapable of doing anything about it ourselves. And that's exactly what He does through the work of the Holy Spirit!

DIVING IN DEEP

Before the foundation of the world, God chose people, the elect, to be His people. He foreknew (which means foreloved) them and predestined them to be saved and to be transformed to be more and more like Jesus. This chosen remnant will come to know and worship God.

What do the following verses say about God's election?

Exodus 33:19

_____

_____

Romans 8:28-30

_____

_____

Romans 9:1-24

_____

_____

Ephesians 1:1-12

_____

_____

2 Thessalonians 2:13-14

_____

_____

Jesus reiterates this. He tells us that the Father has given Him a group of chosen people. These are the people whom He will come to save. They are His sheep who will respond to His voice, spoken through the Gospel proclamation. Jesus will lose none of those given to Him by the Father. This was the Father's will and what was agreed upon by the Trinity before the foundation of the world.

What does Jesus say in the following verses?

John 6:36-40

_____

_____

John 10:23-30

_____

_____

John 17

_____

_____

If this is the first time you've heard this, and you are struggling with it, you're not alone. From a human perspective, this seems unfair—that God would choose to save some, but not all. But the truth is, because all men are deserving of God's wrath and Hell, it is remarkably merciful that He chose to save anyone. We are saved by grace. The definition of *grace* is "unmerited favor."[2] If we did anything at all to earn our own salvation, even making a "choice," it would then become merited and no longer be grace. It is God's electing love that saves, and nothing else.

Read **Ezekiel 11:19**, **36:22-32** *and answer the following questions:*

Who is doing all of the work in this passage?

_____

_____

What specific things is God going to do to His people?

_____

_____

---

2   *The New Strong's Exhaustive Concordance, s.v.* "Grace," Nashville, TN: Thomas Nelson Publishers, 1965.

What is the reason He's going to do these things?

_____

_____

What does He say about Israel (and thus, the Church) in v. 31?

_____

_____

*Read **Acts 16:14.** What happened to Lydia's heart so that she could hear the Gospel?*

_____

_____

*Read **Ephesians 2:1-9** and answer the following questions:*
What do these verses say God does?

_____

_____

What was the human condition before that?

_____

_____

When did He make us alive?

_____

_____

_____

What does it say we are saved by in verses 8-9?

_____

_____

_____

If you are a Christian and never heard this before, does knowing that God chose you to be His and that it wasn't your choosing Him change how you feel about Him? Does it make you love Him more? Does it make you humbler? Does knowing this make you have more compassion for the unsaved?

What happens to those whom God has chosen? At some point in their life, the Holy Spirit regenerates their hearts, which gives them the ability to respond to the Gospel message when they hear it. That's why we preach it, tell it, spread it—to reach the elect! We'll talk more about this later. But for now, we've seen that we are chosen by God. Next, we see that Jesus dies for the people of God, but not for the reasons some think He did.

S-I-N is the Reason Jesus Suffered and Died

In churches all around the world, preachers are claiming that Jesus came to do all kinds of things for His people. People are told that Jesus came to give them their "best life now"—to make them healthy and wealthy; to give them power to overcome any obstacle; and, in general, to take care of any hurt, problem, addiction, suffering, and pain. In short, Jesus came to "turn their frowns upside down." Every Sunday, in church after church, people are promised that responding to the call of the Gospel will change all of the bad circumstances in their lives and give them all of their desires, usually with the caveat "if they have enough faith." This "Santa Claus Jesus" is NOT the Jesus of the Bible. And those things are NOT why He came.

Read the following verses and write down what they say about Jesus, blood, and our sin:

Romans 3:10-18

_____

_____

Romans 3:23

_____

_____

Romans 5:6

_____

_____

Hebrews 9:22

_____

_____

Matthew 20:26-28

_____

_____

1 Timothy 2:5-6

_____

_____

What are the dangers to someone who responds to a "Gospel" call that is focused on gaining your "best life now" by coming to Jesus, instead of on sin and separation from God?

_____

_____

_____

From the first animal sacrificed by God to cover Adam and Eve, through the Old Testament sacrifices, to Jesus dying on the cross, we see one thing is needed to pay for sin. Blood. Jesus's blood on the cross paid for the sins of His people. That's the reason He came. He came and took our sin on Himself, shed His blood on the cross, and suffered the penalty of God's wrath in our place. Our sin was imputed to Him. But it was a two-way transaction because His righteousness was imputed to us. He got our sin and punishment, and we got His righteous, so that we can have our relationship with God restored. Talk about the ultimate "unfair" trade!

Jesus' reason for coming to Earth was not just to be our Friend, to save us from loneliness, to make us wealthy, to fulfill our wishes, or just to physically heal us. While He may do some of these things, the reason He came was to be our **Savior.** In other words, He came to fill our **greatest** need—**salvation from God's wrath**. Although there is more we are promised than forgiveness of sins (i.e. eternal life with Him, a new Heaven and Earth, etc.), we are not promised that if we have faith and trust in His perfect righteousness for salvation that our lives will be better in all the earthly-minded ways we would like them to be. In fact, if we are His, we are promised the opposite.

Read the following verses, and write what they say about the Christian's life:

Philippians 1:29-30

_____

_____

2 Corinthians 1:2-10

_____

_____

James 1:2

_____

_____

Romans 8:35-36

_____

_____

Freed to Live Righteously

If you are trusting in Jesus for forgiveness of your sin, you've been freed! You've been freed to live without the burden of guilt caused by your sin. But you're also freed in another way. You are freed to live righteously. As believers, we are finally free to do what we ought to do. Up to that point, we are in bondage to sin; but from salvation on, we have the ability to choose to live righteously by having a heart inclined to please God. Your chains are broken, and you're made alive and set free!

What do the following verses say?

Romans 6:6

_____

_____

Galatians 5:24

_____

_____

Ephesians 4:22-24

_____

_____

Colossians 3:7-10

_____

_____

Knowing that God chose to save you from before the foundations of the world results in thankfulness and joy, which leads to obedience. When you realize what He did for you, you want to please Him! None of us will do it perfectly in this life; and until we're with Jesus forever, the struggle with our old nature will still be there. But once we become Christians, we will want to live according to our new nature more and more.

How do you feel knowing that you have this freedom?

_____

_____

_____

Does the idea that you can become more and more like Jesus seem impossible to you?

_____

_____

_____

Do you wonder why God does it this way? Do you wonder why He doesn't just make us perfectly like Jesus all at once?

_____

_____

_____

BACK ON DRY LAND

Remember, the point of this study, just like in the book *No Half-Truths Allowed,* is to make sure we have a solid understanding of the whole Gospel message. It's important that the message we understand is that we can't do anything to save ourselves, that God does the saving from start to finish. This is what leads to thankfulness and our desire to glorify Him by our obedience. We also need to know that Jesus came to save us from God's wrath because of our sin, and not to give us a happy, healthy, wealthy life. Believing anything less ourselves, or offering someone else anything but a way to get rid of their sin and have a relationship with their Creator, isn't offering them the Gospel. It may sound good; but it's not the Gospel! Tell them the bad news, and the Good News will sound even better.

Do you know anyone who may have "accepted Jesus" based on false ideas of what the Gospel really is and what Jesus has done? If so, what can you do about it?

_____

_____

Have you or someone you know been waiting for Jesus to change the earthly circumstances of your life (your health, finances, marriages, etc.) based on a false proclamation of what you have been taught that the Gospel is?

_____

_____

_____

The idea of freedom from our guilt sounds amazing, but sometimes the idea of being sanctified to become more and more like Jesus sounds like an insurmountable task. However, if we are Christians, we should take comfort in the fact that the Holy Spirit is working inside of us and doing it in His own timing. Plus, He is the One Who is actually giving us the ability to strive against our sin. That should bring us comfort. In fact, it should give us renewed hope.

If you are a believer, are you free from the weight of guilt from your sin? If not, have you repented and asked God to forgive you? If you have, you really can trust that He forgives you!

_____

_____

_____

Do you see evidence that the Holy Spirit is working inside of you? Do you feel better knowing that you'll be changed in His timing and that it isn't all up to you alone?

_____

_____

_____

SUMMARY

In Ezekiel, God promised to put a new heart and a new spirit in His people, to remove "the heart of stone" and to give us "a heart of flesh" (Ezek. 36:26)! As we, His people, go through this life, He is going to sanctify us, which means to make us more and more like Jesus.

We can take comfort in the fact that we don't have to "go it alone." When we become Christians, the Holy Spirit comes to live inside us. He is our Helper. And He is the One Who's going to work out the bad stuff and turn our hearts more and more toward being God-pleasers. It won't happen completely in this life, but it will start to happen. It won't always be pretty, and it might be painful sometimes; in fact, it *is* going to be painful sometimes. But it is for our good and for His glory.

NOTES

1 + 1 = 1

GETTING YOUR TOES WET

Now that we understand our sin is not just the little mess-ups we have, but a serious offense against God and deserving of eternal punishment, we can move on to the most amazing part of the Gospel message—Jesus saves His people! While it is not unbelievable that we constantly and continually offend God by breaking His precepts and commands, it *is* unbelievable that God, the Son, would want to leave Heaven and come to Earth to pay the penalty for those offenses.

As we did with God the Almighty Father, and as we will do with the Holy Spirit, let's get a foundational understanding of Who Jesus is.

How would you explain what Jesus being fully Man and fully God means to a non-believer or a new believer?

_____

_____

Do you think being fully God made it easier for Jesus to be a human? Why or Why not?

_____

_____

What do you think your resurrected body will look like?

_____

_____

DIVING IN DEEP

Jesus—Fully Man / Fully God

No Bible-believing Christian would argue that Jesus became man when He was born of Mary. But how deeply have we thought about this? Jesus became a human in every way (well, every way but one—more on that in a moment). This is called the Doctrine of the Incarnation.

Incarnation means "the embodiment of a diety or spirit in some earthly form."[3] You may not need to see Scriptural proof that Jesus became fully man but remember rule number one of biblical exegesis. Everything must be backed up by Scripture.

How do these verses substantiate the Doctrine of the Incarnation?

John 1:14

_____

_____

1 Timothy 3:16

_____

_____

Hebrews 2:14

_____

_____

Jesus had to be fully human to be the substitutionary Atonement and reconcile His people with God. Since we, as humans, are the ones under penalty for our sin, only another Human could take that penalty for us. You may be thinking, "But wait, in the Old Testament, they sacrificed animals to pay the penalty for people's sins." This is true, but the reason they had to keep repeating the sacrifices was because an animal sacrifice was insufficient and could never be a permanent substitute for us.

Yes, Jesus needed to be fully human, but He also needed to be fully God, so He could defeat Satan and death. Jesus being fully God is part of the Doctrine of the Trinity we looked at in Lesson 2.

How do these verses validate that Jesus is fully God?

John 10:30-33

_____

_____

John 13:3

_____

_____

---

3   *Merriam-Webster, s.v.* "Incarnation," Accessed March 01, 2019, https://www.merriam-webster.com/dictionary/incarnation.

Colossians 2:9

_____

_____

If Jesus had been only a man, He would have not had the power to defeat sin, death, and Satan. If He were only God, He wouldn't have been a satisfactory Sacrifice to pay the price for our sins. This is why Jesus is the only One who could ever be the Savior!

1 + 1 = 1

Probably all orthodox Christians believe that Jesus is fully Man and fully God. But let's make sure our understanding is correct. Each nature of Jesus (Man and God) have their own distinct properties. They do not mix and mesh into one nature.

Jesus has always been God. He has and will exist for all eternity as God. He became Man at His birth and will remain Man for all eternity. While Jesus' Divine nature could have easily flown Him to wherever He needed to go or produced a feast when He and His disciples' bellies were growling with hunger, Jesus chose to limit Himself to His human flesh for His own needs. He uses His Deity only when He is meeting the needs of others, healing, exorcising demons, reading the thoughts of the Pharisees to rebuke them, or giving the disciples a glimpse of the glory of God.

Look at these two passages. In what ways do you see Jesus confining Himself to His Humanity and in what ways do you see Him displaying His Divinity?

John 11:33-44

_____

_____

Mark 4:35-39

_____

_____

We said earlier that Jesus had to be human to pay the penalty for sin for humans but that He chose to confine Himself to His humanity, so He could experience everything we experience and thereby be able to empathize with us.

Jesus was Human in every aspect except one: He was not born with a sin nature. Remember that Adam and Eve were born without a sin nature? One of the curses for Adam and Eve's failure to obey God was that every human being from then on would be born with a sin nature.

However, in order for Jesus to succeed where Adam failed, He had to start in the same place. Therefore, He, too, was born without a sin nature.

Read Genesis 3:1-7 and Luke 4:1-12.

In a direct contrast to Genesis 3, Luke 4 gives an account of Jesus being tempted by Satan. Unlike the first Adam, the second Adam, Jesus, succeeds. Jesus does not take what was "good for food," but says that "man shall not live by bread alone." Jesus was not lured by what was a "delight to the eyes" when presented with "all of the kingdoms of the world." Jesus says, "Worship the Lord your God, and him only shall you serve." And lastly, Jesus was not fooled by what would "make one wise" when Satan suggested that He throw Himself down from the pinnacle of the temple. Jesus says, "You shall not put the Lord your God to the test." The sin of first Adam led to the condemnation of all, but the righteousness of the second Adam leads to the justification and life for all men who are called by God.

BACK ON DRY LAND

How Jesus' two natures, fully God and fully Man, interact is a mystery. One that our finite minds cannot possibly fully understand. And while it is probably obvious to most that Jesus was, is, and always will be fully God, some may not realize that from the day He was born to Mary, He was and will always be fully Man. While it is because He is fully God that He was able to be resurrected on the third day after His crucifixion, He was resurrected physically in the same body He had been walking around in for thirty-three years while on Earth. Just to clarify, though, while it was the same physical body, it was a resurrected body. Jesus still bore the scars from the crucifixion, but He did not still have the bloody wounds. His body was completely healed. Look at this verse from **Acts 1:9**: *"And when he had said these things, as they were looking on, he was lifted up, and a cloud took him out of their sight."* Jesus physically ascended into Heaven! And once in Heaven, He kept His physical body. How do we know this?

_____

_____

Turn to **Revelation 1:7.** *How does this verse prove Jesus will return in His physical body?*

_____

_____

This is great news for us! If Jesus' physical body was resurrected after death, this means ours will be, too! And like Jesus' resurrected body, ours will be the same, but better. No infirmities nor physical limitations—sort of the 2.0 version of us! Let's look at the following verses. From them, how can we conclude, with certainty, that we, too, will be raised physically like Jesus?

John 5:28-29

_____

_____

1 Corinthians 15:52

_____

_____

1 Thessalonians 4:16

_____

_____

SUMMARY

Certainly, no Person of the Trinity is preached, taught, or sung about more than Jesus. But we need to make sure we have the correct understanding of Who Jesus is and what He actually did for us. Sadly, Jesus is often reduced to an effeminate, romance novel cover model who walks around stroking His pet lamb. He is often thought of as the kinder God—not like the God from the Old Testament, Who was mean. This is most assuredly NOT the Jesus we meet in the Bible. When we get a true, foundational understanding of Who He is, both from the Old Testament and the New Testament, we see that He is exactly like the God from the Old Testament because He is the God from the Old Testament! And far from mean, He is gracious, merciful, and loving, while at the same time being just, righteous, and holy! This is the Jesus Who was prophesied about and promised to the people of God throughout the Old Testament. Next, we will take a look at those promises!

NOTES

_____

_____

_____

_____

PROMISES KEPT

GETTING YOUR TOES WET

What is your favorite song / hymn about Jesus?

_____

_____

What message does it conveys about Jesus?

_____

_____

Do you think it's important to analyze the words of hymns / songs for theological correctness? Why or Why not?

_____

_____

There are so many beautiful songs about Jesus. There are also many incorrect songs about Him! There are popular songs that say things like Jesus didn't want heaven without us. There is a major problem with this. The Trinity is already perfect in Their relationship with each Other and perfect in Heaven. This line makes it sound like Jesus is not happy in Heaven because we are not there. He is completely and perfectly happy without us! The Trinity decided in Their gracious mercy to save a people unto Themselves. Not because they *needed* us to fill emotional voids They have, but just because They *wanted* to!

The name *Jesus* means "God saves." The name *Christ* means "anointed deliverer." So, Jesus Christ means "God saves through an anointed deliverer." God saves us because it is His pleasure to do so, not because there is anything special about us. The people of the Old Testament understood this. Thus, when the Messiah was prophesied about throughout the Old Testament, they understood that God was going to do a miraculous work on their behalf.

DIVING IN DEEP

Jesus Christ the Promised Messiah

Jesus is promised, prophesied, and foreshadowed throughout the Old Testament, beginning back in **Genesis 3:15**. In fact, Genesis 3:15 is called "the first Gospel."

Read this verse. What is God foreshadowing about Jesus?

_____

_____

The amazing promise contained in this verse and others is that we—if we belong to Jesus—get to share in His victory!

How do these New Testament verses attest to that?

_____

_____

1 John 5:3-5

_____

_____

Romans 8:31-32

_____

_____

Ephesians 6:10-13

_____

_____

So often, people misinterpret verses of Scripture like these to mean that with God, you can achieve all of your personal goals or that God will give you success in whatever you do. This is not what these verses are saying!

What is the victory we are promised?

_____

_____

_____

_____

Why He Came When He Did

God could have sent Jesus right after the fall of Adam and Eve. But He didn't. Instead, God waited approximately four thousand more years. Four thousand years of God's people disobeying Him and being cursed for it. Four thousand years of the Israelites trying to make amends with God and repenting for their sin. Four thousand years of God showing mercy on them and saving them. Why didn't He just send Jesus right after the Fall and be done with it?

The main reason for the Old Testament is to show that people cannot possibly save themselves from the wrath of God and that they need a perfect Savior to do it for them. The entire Old Testament points to Jesus! The theme of the Old Testament can be summed up as a picture of God's mercy and grace on His people that would ultimately come to fulfillment in Jesus Christ.

God waited four thousand years to send Jesus. We, on this side of history, have the privilege of seeing how desperate and desolate the world was without Jesus, without having to actually experience it. For God's people who lived up until Jesus' physical coming, they had to cling to the promises of the coming Messiah given to them through God's prophets.

Compare these Old Testament and New Testament verses. *How does the New Testament verse show Jesus fulfilled the Old Testament promise?*

Zechariah 9:9 and Luke 19:35-37

_____

_____

Isaiah 53:4-6 and Romans 3:23-26

_____

_____

Daniel 7:13-14 and Acts 7:55-56

_____

_____

These, and many other prophecies about Jesus, always had a common theme. They were meant to give hope to the people when they most needed it. They were meant to show that God had an ultimate plan for the salvation of His people.

God chose the perfect time in history to send Jesus to the earth. We know it was the perfect time because everything God does is perfect. Ironically, it was also one of the most violent, barbaric times in history. While it may seem strange to us, He did it because the abuse and torture Jesus endured is a picture of how sinful man feels toward God.

Turn to Isaiah 59. *How do verses **Isaiah 59:1-8** show how our sinful nature is at war with God?*

_____

_____

Promises Kept

When we understand that everything in the Old Testament points to Jesus, we read it in a whole new light! We can't help but see Jesus throughout the narratives. It has been noted that there are 574 passages in the Old Testament that prophecy about the coming of Jesus. That is not even including all of the pictures and foreshadowing of Him, nor all of the spiritual and physical appearances of Him (called Theophanies).

Here are a few. *How do these verses illustrate, foreshadow, or promise the coming of Jesus?*

Numbers 21:4-9

_____

_____

Isaiah 9:6-7

_____

_____

Daniel 2:44

_____

_____

With all of the prophecies, promises, appearances, and foreshadowing of Jesus, you would think the Jewish people, especially the Pharisees who had most of the Old Testament memorized, would have recognized Jesus as the Messiah and fallen down before Him to worship Him. But they didn't because they misunderstood the Scripture of the Old Testament. The Jewish people had been oppressed and ruled by various nations for hundreds of years. Some of them had an expectation that the Messiah was coming to deliver them from their current circumstances. They were looking for a warrior King who would defeat their enemy, the Roman Empire. They did not understand that Jesus' Kingdom was not of this world.

We on this side of the resurrection know that Jesus came to save *all* of His people for all eternity, not just the Jewish people in 28-31 A.D. Even after spending three years with Him,

His apostles didn't fully grasp what Jesus' mission was. It wasn't until after they received the Holy Spirit at Pentecost that they understood. Thankfully, they were inspired to record Jesus' exact mission for us in the New Testament.

What do these verses say Jesus' mission on Earth was?

Matthew 26:26-28

_____

_____

Mark 10:45

_____

_____

Romans 5:8-11

_____

_____

BACK ON DRY LAND

What Jesus did for us on the cross is called Substitutionary Atonement. This means Christ died on the cross as our Substitute. Without Him, we would suffer the death and damnation penalty for our own sins. God forsook His own Son so that He might never have to forsake His children.

There are some who struggle with this part of the Gospel. They don't want to believe that they were so bad, they couldn't save themselves, and Someone had to die in their place. This is why the complete Gospel message is so important. Unless a person understands how sinful they are, they will never be able to accept that Jesus had to die in their place.

Jesus died on the cross because He was the only satisfactory Sacrifice that could reconcile sinful man to a holy God. Think of two cliffs across from each other. On the one side is us, and on the other is God. Between the two is a huge, deep chasm that is impossible to cross. Jesus is the only Bridge big enough to cover that chasm. Because of His taking our punishment, we can walk across the bridge and approach our Heavenly Father.

We mustn't end there though! As beautiful as this picture is, we can't end with Jesus' sacrificial death. We must include His resurrection. If Jesus hadn't been resurrected, He would have just been another great teacher or perhaps a prophet who was martyred. Jesus' resurrection changed everything! Jesus' resurrection not only shows He was fully God, but it seals His victory over sin, death, and Satan! And for those of us who are in Him, His victory has been imputed to us.

Jesus' resurrection also shows us that God's perfect justice will prevail. God will always triumph over evil! As we looked at in Lesson 5, Jesus' resurrection also means that just as His physical body both died and rose again, so will ours.

Finally, the resurrection of Jesus initiated the coming of the Holy Spirit, Who indwells in believers. We will look at the Holy Spirit in depth in Lesson 8, but we who have the Holy Spirit living in us have more spiritual fortitude than anyone in the Old Testament, including Moses, David, and the Prophets.

SUMMARY

Hopefully, after these last two studies on Jesus, we have gotten that girly, shampoo model Jesus out of our minds forever and have replaced Him with Who He actually is—our holy, just, omniscient, omnipotent, omnipresent, merciful, and loving Savior, Who forsook His own glory, came to Earth to be born in humble circumstances, lived a perfect life, suffered abominable torture, and ultimately, willingly died a horrific death so we could spend eternity with Him in Heaven.

You may wonder what Jesus' motivation was. **Hebrews 12:2** gives us the answer: *"Looking to Jesus, the founder and perfecter of our faith, who for the joy that was set before him endured the cross, despising the shame, and is seated at the right hand of the throne of God."* Friends, if you belong to Jesus, the reason He came to Earth was for you! You were the joy set before Him! When we get this, how could we possibly grow weary and lose heart? As Chapter 12 in Hebrews continues in verse three, *"Consider him who endured from sinners such hostility against himself, so that you may not grow weary or fainthearted."*

NOTES

_____
_____
_____
_____
_____
_____
_____

AND THE ANSWER IS . . .

GETTING YOUR TOES WET

What comes to your mind when you see the word "believe" by itself on a plaque or other decoration?

_____

_____

Have you ever expressed that you're worried or stressed about something and had someone respond to you, "Just have faith, and everything will work out fine"? How would you take it if you were in that situation? If you've had that happen, how did it make you feel?

_____

_____

What does the word "repentance" mean to you?

_____

_____

Now that we've learned about Jesus, the Lamb of God Who takes away our sins, the One Who was our substitute Who took the wrath of God upon Himself in our place, the next logical question is, "What do I need to do in order to be saved? The question that follows after that one for some is "What *don't* I have to do to be saved?" Hopefully, after this lesson, you will see the importance of knowing the answers to these two questions—both for yourself and for others.

DIVING IN DEEP

The Chosen are Regenerated and Called

Like we've said before, God's elect will at some point in their lives have their hearts of stone regenerated and turned to flesh, a work done by the Holy Spirit. At that point, our hearts are ready to respond to the Gospel call when we hear it! The Gospel call is not a calling like a job calling, such as "being called into ministry" or something like that. Instead, it is the proclamation of the Gospel message calling out to all people the Good News of what Jesus has done. The Gospel call goes out to all people, and those whose hearts have been regenerated will respond. We call this "effectual calling."

Human preaching and teaching is the way the general call of the Gospel goes forth. It is the way God's elect hear His call so that they can respond and come to Him. That's why we have to be obedient and spread the Gospel message. *How do these verses illustrate this?*

Isaiah 55:11

_____

_____

1 Thessalonians 1:4-5

_____

_____

2 Thessalonians 2:13-14

_____

_____

Acts 13:46-47

_____

_____

Acts 16:13-14

_____

_____

1 Corinthians 1:23-31

_____

_____

Like we have said before, not all Gospel calls are effective. The job of believers is to explain the Gospel message, but it is up to God whether that message or call is effectual. It's important to understand that we are *not* responsible for "getting anyone saved," nor are we responsible if someone dies without any evidence of salvation. We spread the Gospel out of obedience to God because we love Him, not because the pastor made us feel guilty that someone we love never made a profession of faith before they died, as if it was our fault. The doctrine of election is something we can take comfort in and help others take comfort in, when we're talking about the possible salvation of those who cannot make a profession of faith on their own, including those who cannot hear or understand the Gospel and the unborn. When it is God doing the saving from start to finish, we have the hope that anyone might be one of the elect.

But getting back to the response to the Gospel call, what exactly is that response? We usually hear two words associated with that response: Faith and Repentance.

"And the Answer Is . . . Faith Alone (Sola Fide) in Christ's Work Alone (Solo Christo)!"

Faith is, in general, the firm persuasion that a certain statement is true. But its primary idea here is trust. The Gospel is true, and therefore worthy of our trust. Having faith in the Gospel message is having a total reliance on (a total trust in) the fact that God will accept Jesus' sacrifice for your sin in your place. It is a reliance that is not "upheld" in your mind by your good deeds, your Bible study, or anything else. You are *totally* counting on what Jesus did on the cross to pay for your sins. You are coming to God empty-handed! This is what the patriarchs, our forefathers (and mothers) of the faith, did. *Read Hebrews 11:1-13.*

The greatest need of every human is that when we stand before God, He declares us "righteous" and not "condemned." When we trust in Jesus' death on the cross as atonement for our sin, we are declared righteous by God. *What do the following verses have to say about this?*

Isaiah 53:4-6

_____

_____

Romans 4:13

_____

_____

Romans 5:6-8

_____

_____

2 Corinthians 5:21

_____

_____

1 Peter 3:18

_____

_____

This faith is the lone instrument of justification (being made in right relationship with God). *What is the basis for our salvation in these verses?*

Romans 3:20-24

_____

_____

Romans 4:5-8

_____

_____

Romans 5:1

_____

_____

Philippians 3:8-9

_____

_____

Justification is an instantaneous event that results in a permanent change of our status before God. Just like when a child is adopted into a family, the very moment the papers are signed and the adoption is final, the child is now a full-fledged member of the family. His status has changed *permanently*.

Does this give us a license to sin, knowing that we'll be forgiven, which is called antinomianism? Certainly not! We are called to live righteously, and to cooperate with the Holy Spirit to mortify our sin. *Read **Romans 6:13-18**. What does Paul say about this?*

_____

_____

But What About Repentance?

There's some debate about whether you need more than faith in Jesus' perfect life, His death as payment for your sins, and His resurrection to actually be saved. The thing most often debated about is *repentance*. Do you need repentance, as well as faith, in order to be saved? The truth is, there really shouldn't be much to debate about. If you are truly saved, you will want to repent of your sin. Repentance, like faith, is a fruit of being regenerated.

What is repentance? It is more than just asking God for forgiveness. It is really like doing a 180-degree turn from your sin, so that your life is lived differently. Picture the difference of your heart of stone that is changed to a heart of flesh. The fruit of our lives after we've repented should reflect that change.

Read the following verses calling for repentance, and write down some key words or phrases having to do with repentance:

Job 42:1-6

_____

_____

2 Kings 22:9

_____

_____

Matthew 4:17

_____

_____

Acts 3:19

_____

_____

Acts 26:20

_____

_____

A Christian will begin to hate his sin. He will be grieved over it because he realizes he's offended God. He will cooperate more and more with the Holy Spirit to mortify it. This will be a true feeling of remorse at having offended God. If you've been saved by Jesus, you will begin to live a life of repentance as you're convicted of sin.

In an opposite sort of way, there is a type of repentance motivated by remorse, self-reproach, and sorrow for sin, generated by a fear of punishment or realization of bad consequence caused by your sins. This is called attrition or "false repentance" because there is no sign of sorrow for having offended God, and it is lacking in any true appeal for His forgiveness. This repentance shows no true desire to turn from that sin or to rid yourself of it.

Compare David's reaction to his sin in Psalm 51:3-4 and that of the prodigal son in Luke 15:21 with Esau's behavior and attitude in Genesis 25:29-34, 27:30-41 and Hebrews 12:16-17. What differences do you see?

_____

_____

David and the prodigal son have true remorse at having offended the Father. But Esau is only sad because he's realized what he's lost, the bad consequences he's going to suffer, and that it's too late to change things. He demonstrates only anger and frustration over what his sin has cost him, but that is the only reason he's sorry.

Many churches today offer alter calls and open baptisms (baptism offered to anyone who wants to come forward at that time, without prior meeting with the pastors/leaders), sometimes without even having preached the complete message of the Gospel beforehand.

Do you see how someone could gain a false idea that they are saved by going forward for the altar call or baptism in this type of situation? How can pastors and church leadership do this in a better way?

_____

_____

But What About Baptism, Good Works, and Speaking in Tongues? Don't I Have to Do These to be Saved?

There is nowhere in the Bible that expresses that idea that baptism saves. *Read 1 **Corinthians 1:17**. What does this verse say Paul was sent to do?*

_____

_____

The Bible does not say we need good works to be saved. *Read: **2 Timothy 1:8-9** and **Titus 3:4-7**. What do they say about being saved by our works?*

_____

_____

Some people claim that at some point after being saved, you must speak in "tongues" to prove your salvation. We will look at why in "Back on Dry Land." Often, when mentioned in this context, what is meant is a strange, unintelligible kind of babbling. There are even pastors who claim they can teach you how to do it. Let's take a look at what the Bible has to say about the gift of tongues with the following passages of Scripture.

*What are the people of different nations hearing according to **Acts 2:4-11**?*

_____

_____

*How many tongues gifts are mentioned in **1 Corinthians 12:10**? What are they?*

_____

_____

*Who is supposed to benefit from the spiritual gifts given to the church according to **1 Peter 4:10** and **1 Corinthians 12:4-7**?*

_____

_____

_____

Paul says a good deal about the use of tongues to the Corinthian church in **1 Corinthians 14.** From the text, we can see that tongues was used in corporate worship to edify the believers, just like the rest of the spiritual gifts. But in order for tongues to build up the church, it must be interpreted. If someone used the gift and no one within earshot could understand, the person was basically only "talking to God," and no one would be edified except the speaker himself. If the tongue was interpreted, it would be useful to the whole body, just like speaking the Word of God (prophesying) was useful. But if no one could understand what the speaker was saying, it profited nothing.

None of these things mentioned above needs to be done to inherit salvation, nor does any of them need to be done to prove salvation. Over and over again, Jesus Himself told people it was their *faith* that saved them. *What does Jesus say saves in the following verses?*

Matthew 9:2

_____

_____

Matthew 9:22

_____

_____

Mark 10:52

_____

_____

Luke 8:48

_____

_____

BACK ON DRY LAND

Christians throughout history have tied these three things—baptism, works, and speaking in tongues—to faith, either as something needed in order to be saved, or something needed as proof of salvation. Often this comes from the contested verses of Mark 16:9-20. While there is much to be said about these verses, in short, there is no agreed upon way that Mark ended his Gospel. Some say he ended at verse eight because these verses are not found in the earliest manuscripts and because they are a different style and vocabulary from the rest. Some say verses nine through twenty are worth consideration. They say it is found on fragments of other manuscripts, and the difference in style and vocabulary is because it wasn't authored by Mark but was authored by someone else with apostolic approval. There are other ideas about this passage also. ***Read Mark 16:9-20.***

If we consider these verses as Scripture, we see that Jesus is instructing His eleven apostles here, just as we see elsewhere. We also know that there were instances in the early church of instantaneous healing, miracles, and speaking and interpreting of languages previously unknown to the speaker; and, of course, we know that there were baptisms. There is no record of believers drinking poison and surviving in the New Testament, but there are records of miraculous healings. In the same way, there is no record of intentional snake-handling by believers, although Paul was bitten by a poisonous snake on the island of Malta, and he lived. Regarding baptism, we see nowhere else in Scripture that in order to be saved, you must be baptized or that baptism itself saves anyone.

There are some other things to consider in addition. First, the things listed in Mark 16 are *descriptive* not *prescriptive*. There is no *demand* to engage in these practices; it only says that some believers *will* have these things happen.

Second, there is good reason to believe that the apostolic gifts (miracles, instantaneous healing, speaking in tongues, being able to interpret tongues, and prophecy) are no longer functioning today. This is referred to as the Cascade Argument; and the cascade, in short, goes like this: 1) There are no apostles of Christ on Earth today. 2) Because there are no apostles today, there are no prophets. 3) Because there are no prophets, there are no tongue-speakers. 4) Because of one through three, there are no miracle-workers on Earth today.

Christ's apostles were not just followers. They had three distinguishing marks: they had to be directly appointed by Christ (that's why the lot was cast to replace Judas Iscariot); they had to be a physical eyewitness to the resurrected Jesus; and they had to do miracles. *What do the following verses tell us about the apostles?*

Matthew 10:1-7

_____

_____

Mark 3:14

_____

_____

Luke 6:13

_____

_____

Acts 1:1-3

_____

_____

Although we tend to think of prophecy as "telling the future"—and it often was predictive—in reality, it was a telling of what God had revealed to the prophet, whether past, present, or future. *Read **Numbers 12:2**, **Deuteronomy 13:1-5**, **and Amos 3:7** and answer the following questions:*

Who gave the prophets the words they were to say?

_____

_____

In light of the first question, what was the job of a prophet?

_____

_____

What was the penalty for speaking something false?

_____

_____

*What were the prophets in the New Testament doing, and what do the following verses tell us about what their purpose was for the believers in **Ephesians 4:11-12** and **1 Corinthians 14:3**? For unbelievers in **1 Corinthians 14:24-25**?*

_____

_____

The prophets were "proclaimers of a divine message." In other words, true prophets spoke the words of God. According to Ephesians 2:20, the Church is built on the foundation of the apostles and prophets, with Christ as the Chief Cornerstone. *Consider the following:*

*How does **Hebrews 1:1-2** tell us God spoke in these last days?*

_____

_____

*What does **Revelation 1:1-2** say the Book of Revelation is?*

_____

_____

*What do **Deuteronomy 4:2, 12:32**, and **Revelation 22:18-19** say?*

_____

_____

Logically speaking, if prophets spoke the words God gave them to speak, and we're told that in the last days God spoke through Jesus, then we know that Jesus had the **last** words to say. And He did—in the book of Revelation, and that would mean there's no new revelation from God since then.

Like we said with this general overview of the cascade theory, if there are no more apostles and no more Prophets, then there's no more gift of tongues or the other apostolic gift. They were useful for getting the Church started but would have ceased sometime in the very early Church.

If the gift of tongues is still active today, some would say it's for use in private prayer to God. Since we've seen from the above verses that spiritual gifts were for building up the

Church, not for private use, that may not be the case. However, either way, **for the purpose we've been talking about regarding salvation**, it is *not* needed in order *to be saved*, nor for *proof of salvation*. To say that it's needed flies in the face of the rest of Scripture.

SUMMARY

"Faith Alone (Sola Fide) in Christ's Work Alone (Solo Christo)" was the cry of the Reformers during the Protestant Reformation. When we share the Gospel message, we need to make sure that nothing gets left out, nor added to it! We want to make sure that people understand what the Scriptures teach regarding salvation so that no one walks away with a false sense of security, as well as insuring that no one is living their Christian life afraid that there are requirements for salvation or proof of salvation that they haven't met yet.

NOTES

_____

_____

_____

_____

_____

_____

_____

_____

_____

_____

_____

_____

_____

_____

_____

_____

_____

_____

_____

Lesson 8

THE MULTI-TASKER

GETTING YOUR TOES WET

What are some things that you know or have heard about the Holy Spirit?

_____

_____

Do you believe that someone who is saved can lose their salvation? Why or why not?

_____

_____

_____

Have you ever known someone who is a believer, but then found out about some very sinful behavior they've been doing? If so, did it make you question their salvation? As a Christian, has your sin ever made you question your own salvation?

_____

_____

_____

Just as we need to have a foundational understanding of Who God the Father and Jesus the Son are, we need to also understand Who the Holy Spirit is and how He functions within the Trinity. The Holy Spirit is the third Person of the Trinity. He is responsible for many different works in the life of a believer—some of which we've mentioned already, but we will take a deeper look at His work in this lesson.

DIVING IN DEEP

The Work of the Holy Spirit

Like we've said, the Holy Spirit is responsible for many different tasks in the life of the believer. *Read the following verses and write down some of the ways we see the Holy Spirit working:*

Genesis 1:2

_____

_____

2 Samuel 23:2

_____

_____

Micah 3:8

_____

_____

Exodus 35:30-31

_____

_____

Mark 13:11

_____

_____

Luke 1:41

_____

_____

John 14:26

_____

_____

2 Peter 1:21

_____

_____

These are just a few examples of what the Holy Spirit does, but you can see why we titled this lesson "The Multi-Tasker"!

Although the Old Testament has a lot to say about the Holy Spirit, it is not made perfectly clear that the Spirit is a distinct Divine Person. It is not until the New Testament that it is clear the Spirit is distinct from the Father and from the Son. This becomes apparent when Jesus promises "another Counselor." It is made clear that the Holy Spirit is a personal Being from the fact that He speaks, teaches, searches, witnesses, determines, can be lied to, and can be grieved.

How do the following passages prove that the Spirit is God?

Acts 5:3-4

_____

_____

Matthew 28:19

_____

_____

2 Corinthians 13:14

_____

_____

The Holy Spirit gives the believer an inward Witness to believe that the Bible is the Word of God! Not only is Scripture authenticated to the believer by Him, but He also opens our minds to be able to understand it! As we saw in Lesson 4, He regenerates the hearts of believers, so they can respond to the Gospel. After that, He works on us from the inside to sanctify us and make us more and more like Christ throughout the rest of our lives.

What do the following passages tell us about Him?

1 Peter 1:2

_____

_____

John 14:26

_____

_____

John 15:26

_____

_____

Romans 8:26

_____

_____

Saved, Sealed, Delivered, We're His!

The Holy Spirit is also our Seal for eternity in Heaven. But the truth is, someone who is truly a Christian can never lose their salvation. How can we be sure of this, when some Christians teach that salvation can be lost?

We start at the beginning with this question: *What state do you believe the human race has been in since Adam and Eve sinned?*

_____

_____

_____

_____

Many people who consider themselves evangelical Christians today believe that salvation is by man's own choice or based on his own moral character. These beliefs usually fall into one of three categories, or sometimes a mixture of the following:

Pelagianism: The belief that Adam's sin did not affect all of humanity; therefore, human beings are born innocent, and it is the freedom of the human will to choose either good or evil. This idea has been condemned by several church councils, and Pelagius was condemned as a heretic and excommunicated in 418 AD.

What do the following verses say that show this is not true?

Romans 3:23; 5:12

_____

_____

1 Corinthians 15:21-22

_____

_____

James 3:2

_____

_____

John 1:8-10

_____

_____

Arminianism: The view that believes every person is depraved, but not totally. This view believes that everyone has a "little bit" of good left in them, that people were only "weakened" by the fall and not spiritually deadened. The belief is that in this state, man is still "good enough" to be able to reach out to God, to respond to His "wooing," to muster up faith in response to the Gospel message. The idea is that man makes the first move. He reaches out to God first; then God gives him grace. This is the prevailing view today.

What do the following verses say that show this is not true?

Deuteronomy 7:6

_____

_____

Deuteronomy 14:2

_____

_____

Isaiah 41:8-9

_____

_____

Romans 8:30

_____

_____

Ephesians 1:3-6

_____

_____

John 5:21

_____

_____

Wesleyanism: The view similar, but different, than Arminianism is the belief that human beings were deadened by the fall of Adam, but that God gave everyone a "little island of grace" (which is known as "Prevenient Grace"). This small amount of grace begins the process of drawing a person to God. It prepares the heart for hearing the Gospel, but it can be resisted. Prevenient Grace is universal, meaning all humans receive it, regardless of their having heard of Jesus.

What do the following verses say that show this is not true?

Exodus 4:21

_____

_____

Deuteronomy 2:30

_____

_____

Joshua 11:20

_____

_____

John 10:25-29

_____

_____

Romans 9:13-18

_____

_____

In Chapter 3, we looked at many parts of Scripture that tell us man is totally dead in his sin, hostile to God, and has no inclination to seek God. Since man is dead, he cannot initiate any part of salvation. God initiates salvation. Why does your view about whether man is dead, just sick and totally depraved, or having an "island of righteousness" make a difference in whether or not you believe salvation can be lost? If you believe that man is responsible for any part of his own salvation, then the logical conclusion is 1) that it's man's option to walk away from his salvation and 2) that he may not ever have done enough to actually secure his salvation. In other words, he may have missed the mark!

On the other hand, if God's electing love is what you believe saved you, then the logical conclusion is to believe that He absolutely will continue to do so. If God has done all of the saving, from start to finish, why wouldn't He bring it to completion?

Read the following verses and what they say about being sealed with the Holy Spirit and salvation:

John 6:37-39

John 17:12

Ephesians 1:13-14

---

2 Thessalonians 2:13-14

Philippians 1:6

There are several Scripture references that seem to say that we can lose our salvation. However, we have to look at them in correct context to get the real meaning. For example, Galatians 5:4 says, "You are severed from Christ, you who would be justified by the law; you have fallen away from grace." It sounds like you can "fall away," but Paul is really just admonishing believers for relying on the law (circumcision) instead of relying solely on Christ. This is an admonishment against works-based salvation; he's not saying those who truly believe can lose their salvation. Some other Scriptures like this are Colossians 1:22-23, James 5:19-20, and 2 Peter 2:20-22.

Goats Among Sheep

When Jesus comes again, He will separate out the unbelievers (goats) from the elect/believers (sheep), as we see in Matthew 25:31-46. We attend worship services every week as a mixed group of sheep and goats. Not everyone who goes to church is really saved. These "goats" may experience blessings from God because of their close association with the faithful; but in the end, they will suffer eternal judgment. There are even many who will speak and act no different from a true believer.

The books of 1 John and Jude (as well as many others) warn about false teachers who had been of the church. *Read what they have to say about them in **1 John 2:19** and **Jude 1:4**, along with what John says about true believers in **1 John 2:23-25**.*

John tells us that those people "were not of us," and Jude tells us they "long ago were designated for this condemnation." These were ungodly people from the start. They were not believers who lost their salvation.

BACK ON DRY LAND

Perseverance or Preservation?

The theological point we've been talking about is called "the Perseverance of the Saints." It is more accurate to think of it as "God's preserving us," than "us persevering." Reformers have often looked at this in light of both definitions.

*Read **Philippians 2:12-13**, and write down how it reflects our persevering and God's preserving us.*

Just as Paul told the Philippian church in Philippians 1:6, *"And I am sure of this, that he who began a good work in you will bring it to completion at the day of Jesus Christ,"* we know that right now Jesus is sitting at the right hand of God the Father interceding for us. He is our Great High Priest. The writer of Hebrews tells us that His priesthood continues forever and that He is able to "save to the uttermost" in Hebrews 7:25.

It is the Holy Spirit Who raises us to eternal life. God starts our salvation with a promise to finish. The Holy Spirit helps with our preservation. We are sealed, and we are given the Spirit as a down-payment of our salvation. While people may put a down-payment on something and then walk away from it, God never does. Since it is God putting the down-payment on His elect, He is going to preserve those whose names are in the Book of Life—all the way through this life. *Read Paul's words from **Romans 8:34-39**.*

SUMMARY

No believer will be made totally sinless in this lifetime on Earth. It is even possible for truly regenerate believers to fall into gross sin and to backslide in ways that seem incredible to us. The truth is, none of us know what sins we are still capable of doing, even after years or decades of being a Christian. A prime example of this is David, who committed adultery and murder. David sinned grievously but was still called "a man after God's own heart." He may have fallen away from grace, but he never fell out of grace. There are other examples just like him throughout the Scriptures. This is why it is important for a church to have a method for church discipline. Just as Nathan confronted David about his sin, which led him to repentance, the goal of church discipline is to bring an unrepentant member to an acknowledgement of his sin before the Lord and to gently and lovingly encourage him to restore his relationship to God and to fellowship within the Church.

The doctrine of the Perseverance of the Saints is a comfort to saints who are struggling with sin. It is a comfort to the dying, to those who need encouragement, to parents of prodigals, and to every believer. It takes away the questions of whether we've done enough, done it correctly, were sincere enough, or know enough. We don't have to "close the deal." In fact, we never could!

If you are a believer in Christ, nothing can separate you from the love of God. You were chosen before the foundation of the world, bought with the precious blood of Christ, sealed with the Holy Spirit, and someday will be a citizen of Heaven. We really can take comfort in the assurance of our salvation. The Bible tells us so.

NOTES

PRICELESS REWARDS AND ROYAL RESPONSIBILITIES

GETTING YOUR TOES WET

How much thought do you give to the rewards you receive from being a Christian?

_____

_____

How about the responsibilities you have being a Christian?

_____

_____

What are some of the rewards you receive when you become a Christian?

_____

_____

How do these rewards sustain you in your faith?

_____

_____

What are our responsibilities as a Christian?

_____

_____

DIVING IN DEEP

When we are saved, we become children of God and heirs to the Kingdom of God. Maybe you never thought about what that actually means. It means that, as heirs, we become royalty in God's Kingdom. We will explore this in detail in the next lesson. It also means that we have direct access to God the Father and that we have an inheritance. You may remember the story of the rich, young ruler in Mark 10. He asked Jesus what he had to do to inherit eternal life within God's Kingdom. He should have known that inheritance isn't based on what we *do*; it's based on who we are. Inheritance is given to those who are part of the family. And just like our salvation, our inheritance and inclusion in the Kingdom of God can never be lost!

The Kingdom of God is mentioned 126 times in the Gospels and a total of 160 times throughout the New Testament, with most of these references coming directly from Jesus. It bears defining.

While sometimes referred to as the Kingdom of Heaven, the Kingdom of God was part of the central message of Jesus. Throughout the Gospels, we repeatedly see the theme of, *"Repent, for the Kingdom of God is near."* Also, every one of the forty-six different parables Jesus told was about the Kingdom of God!

Defining God's Kingdom is not an easy task. God's Kingdom has always been, is now, and is still to come.

1. **The Kingdom of God has always been.** The Kingdom of God is not a geographical place like the United Kingdom. It can best be defined as God's sovereignty and rule over His people, or, to put it simply, it is **God's redemptive reign**.

    How do these verses illustrate that the Kingdom of God is God's redemptive reign that has always been?

    1 Chronicles 29:11–12

    _____

    _____

    Psalm 145:11-13

    _____

    _____

    Daniel 4:34-35

    _____

    _____

God has always reigned over everything and everyone in the entire universe. His redemptive reign is His reign over His people. Since He chose His people before the creation of the world, He has always had a redemptive reign on them; this means the Kingdom of God existed before the foundation of the world.

2. The Kingdom of God is now. Matthew 3:1-2 shows us that John the Baptist's purpose was to prepare the people for the coming of God's Kingdom on Earth. *"In those days John the Baptist came preaching in the wilderness of Judea, 'Repent, for the kingdom of heaven is at hand.'"* The Kingdom of Heaven, or the Kingdom of God, was coming by and through Jesus. But Jesus didn't just usher in the Kingdom of God; He *is* the Kingdom of God. He is both the King and the Kingdom! Since the time that Jesus has ushered in the Kingdom of God, it has been present on the Earth.

How do these verses show Jesus as the King and/or the Kingdom?

John 12:14-15

_____

_____

John 18:36-37

_____

_____

Colossians 1:13

_____

_____

3. The Kingdom of God has yet to come. Scripture makes it clear that the Kingdom of God has always been and is now. However, if we look at the Lord's Prayer that Jesus taught His disciples in **Matthew 6:5-15** and **Luke 11:1-13**, He tells them to pray, *"Your Kingdom come . . . on earth as it is in heaven."* This implies that there is an aspect of the Kingdom of God that has not yet come to us on Earth and that the ultimate fulfillment of the Kingdom of God on Earth will come only when Jesus comes back. If the Kingdom of God has always been God's redemptive reign and was ushered in and fulfilled by the Incarnate Jesus, what would still be yet to come? *"On earth as it is in heaven"* implies that the Kingdom of God currently on Earth is not the same as the Kingdom of God in Heaven. Just like the ultimate defeat of sin, Satan, and death will occur when Jesus comes back, so will the ultimate fulfillment of God's Kingdom. God's Kingdom on Earth will be just like God's Kingdom in Heaven.

What do these verses say about the Kingdom that is to come?

Matthew 25:31-34

_____

_____

Revelation 21:1-8

_____

_____

Revelation 21:23-27

_____

_____

When Jesus comes back and establishes God's Kingdom on Earth, all hearts will follow Jesus; all mouths will proclaim Him as Lord; and Jesus' enemies will be a footstool beneath His feet.

Royal Responsibilities

Ephesians 2:19-20 says, _"So then you are no longer strangers and aliens, but you are fellow citizens with the saints and members of the household of God, built on the foundation of the apostles and prophets, Christ Jesus himself being the cornerstone."_ **First Peter 2:9** builds on that, saying, _"But you are a chosen race, a royal priesthood, a holy nation, a people for his own possession, that you may proclaim the excellencies of him who called you out of darkness into his marvelous light."_ These verses are telling us that when we belong to God, we become royalty! Being a child of the King means we are all princes and princesses!

We may have fantasized about being a prince or princess when we were children. However, ask any actual royal, and they will tell you that the fantasy doesn't always match the reality. Certainly, there are incredible privileges to being royalty, but there are also incredible responsibilities. For those of us who are children of the one, true King, one responsibility is knowing we are owned by God, purchased by the blood of Jesus, and that we owe ourselves as a living sacrifice to God. That's a mouthful; but put in simpler terms, we are no longer our own boss. Our hearts, our minds, our lives, our very bodies belong to God. We must be ready to serve Him with all of them.

What do these verses say about us belonging to God?

Romans 12:1-2

_____

_____

1 Corinthians 6:17-20

_____

_____

Another responsibility, which stems out of the first, is that we are to be God's witnesses to the world. Mention the words *evangelism* or *witnessing*, and you will see people cringe. It's not that they don't want to serve God; they just don't want to do it in that way. They are happy to make a meal for someone, but please don't ask them to talk about Jesus to someone!

What do these verses say about witnessing?

Psalm 40:9-10

_____

_____

1 Peter 3:15-16

_____

_____

Matthew 28:18-20

_____

_____

BACK ON DRY LAND

Jesus doesn't suggest we witness to people. He doesn't even ask us to witness to people. He *commands* us to witness to people. Even if evangelism is not our strong gift, we need to do it. To refuse would be like refusing to show someone mercy because mercy is not a gift you feel you possess. The good news is that all spiritual gifts can be developed over time and with use. We may start out weak and shaky in our witnessing; but after a while, we will get more comfortable with it and will become more confident doing it.

Romans 1:16 says, *"For I am not ashamed of the gospel, for it is the power of God for the salvation to everyone who believes."* **This was a radical statement Paul was making!** This word "gospel" in the original Greek is a word that was seldom used at the time this was written. Nobody talked this way because the word literally means nearly-too-good-to-be-true news. It referred to news that was so awesome, nothing really justified using it. There was nothing that was too good to be true—that is, until Jesus came along! Which is precisely the point Paul is making.

Because what Jesus did for us is the only thing in all of history worthy of being labeled "gospel," we cannot alter it. We cannot try to avoid feelings of shame or rejection by altering the Gospel message to make it popular and inoffensive. Sadly, this is exactly what many popular "Christian teachers" have done. They have watered down, and sometimes completely altered, the Word of God. They pull verses out of context and use them to make ridiculous claims like, "God wants to give you your best life," or "God will prosper you and make your life happy." Perhaps even worse, there is a highly successful author who claims that Jesus gives her new revelation to pass onto the world. Not only are these "revelations" unbiblical, they don't even sound like anything Jesus would ever say. Friends, this is heresy, and these are lies Satan uses to distract believers from the truth! The only way to combat these lies is to proclaim truth. The only way to proclaim truth is to witness.

SUMMARY

The comfort of the Gospel is what Jesus has done for you. When we set our minds on that—appreciating, rejoicing, and resting in that—we will find strength we never knew we had.

Don't be discouraged when people reject what you tell them. Don't feel guilty if you witness to someone, and they tell you they are not interested. Don't get upset if someone shuts you out of their life because they are angry that you have told them they need to admit they are a sinner and that they need Jesus. When our Gospel message is rejected, it is not us that is being rejected; it is Jesus.

In **2 Corinthians 2:15**, it says, *"For we are the aroma of Christ to God among those who are being saved and among those who are perishing, to one a fragrance from death to death, to the other a fragrance from life to life."* It is not for us to concern ourselves with whom God will save and whom He won't. We are called to be the "aroma of Christ," to reflect the light of God to the world. The rejections will be hard, for sure. It will be painful to see someone we care about reject the Truth. But keep in mind, you don't know what seeds you may be planting. A week, a month, or years from now, that person may come back to what you said and say, "I see it now!" I promise you that when someone does accept your Gospel message and comes to Jesus, when you are the fragrance of life to someone, it will be the most rewarding experience in your life!

NOTES

_____

_____

_____

_____

_____

COUNTING THE COST

GETTING YOUR TOES WET

What are some things you "counted the cost" for before forging ahead with them?

_____

_____

_____

What things can you point to in your life where the benefits have far outweighed the cost?

_____

_____

_____

What are some of the costs you have personally paid in order to follow Jesus?

_____

_____

_____

Everything we do comes with a cost. Sometimes the cost of something is very little; and sometimes, it can be great. Some costs we carefully consider before forging ahead; while others, we may not even give a thought to. When our children are deciding on where to go to college, we sit down and carefully think through the costs of their attending each of their prospective schools: tuition, distance, class offerings, housing, etc. On the other hand, if we just want to paint our bedroom, we probably go buy a can of paint, come home, and start rolling. Often, Christians fall in the latter and do not give any thought about the cost of following Jesus. While counting the cost is not essential to being a believer, having a realistic expectation of what life as a child of God could look like will keep us from becoming disillusioned and disappointed.

DIVING IN DEEP

Following Him / Following Him

In **Luke 14:28-30**, Jesus talks about weighing the cost of being His disciple. He compares it to a building project. *"For which of you, desiring to build a tower, does not first sit down and count the cost, whether he has enough to complete it? Otherwise, when he has laid a foundation and is not able to finish, all who see it begin to mock him, saying, 'This man began to build and was not able to finish.'"* In other words, Jesus is saying if you are going to start following Me, make sure you are prepared to go all the way. Thankfully, He shows us exactly what following Him may cost us.

Read **Luke 9:57-62**. This passage in Luke takes place at the end of Jesus' earthly ministry as He resolutely sets out for Jerusalem knowing He will be crucified and killed there. On the way, He goes through Samaria, but was not welcome there because they found out He was going to Jerusalem. The Jews and the Samaritans were enemies. So, not only was Jesus walking into His own death in Jerusalem; but on the way, He was rejected in Samaria by those who hated Him because of His lineage.

There are two things going on in this passage. For those who follow *Him*, there is the perfect, beautiful Person of Jesus. Nothing could be sweeter. However, in order to follow *Him*, we must also be willing to *follow* Him. *Following* Jesus means taking His path and being willing to risk enduring the same things He had to: rejection (like in Samaria), persecution, and death (like in Jerusalem).

Going back through the passage in Luke 9, what is the situation of each man and how does Jesus respond to him?

1st Man –

_____

_____

2nd Man –

_____

_____

3rd Man –

_____

_____

All three of these accounts have one central message. To be a disciple (*follower*) of Jesus is costly. Jesus is pointing out different possible costs of *following* Him to these men.

Granted, most of us will never lose our home or life because we are *following* Jesus. But there are many that are. It is estimated that there are 30,000 Christians in prison in North Korea being tortured, starved, and killed for offenses such as owning a Bible or publicly speaking about Jesus.[4] So, while those of us in the free world may never face a cost this severe, the point is, we must be *willing* to, if needed. Jesus must be at the center and at the head of our lives. He must always be our top priority, no matter what. He is the Sustainer and Master of the universe. Everything belongs to Him! Yet He willingly temporarily gave up His glory and His majesty to come to Earth as a Man to save us. What He received in return was temptation, rejection, betrayal, heartache, torture, and death. If He was willing to pay all of that for us, is there any sacrifice that would be too great for us to pay for Him?

What do these verses tell us we can expect as followers of Jesus?

Matthew 16:24-25

_____

_____

Romans 14:7-8

_____

_____

1 Peter 4:1-3

_____

_____

Luke 14:26

_____

_____

John 15:20

_____

_____

4   Mike Pence, "Remarks by Vice President Pence at Ministerial To Advance Religious Freedom," (speech, Washington, D.C., July 26, 2018) The White House, https://www.whitehouse.gov/briefings-statements/remarks-vice-president-pence-ministerial-advance-religious-freedom.

2 Timothy 3:12-13

_____

_____

Acts 14:22

_____

_____

Yes, *following* Jesus will be hard at times, but He never asks us to do it alone. Truth is, we never could do it alone. None of us are that strong on our own. It is only when we *follow* in the power of the Holy Spirit that we will be able to withstand any costs. This is true whether it is being ridiculed for our faith, being rejected by our family and friends, forfeiting our possessions, or even losing our lives.

Why would anyone be willing to pay the costs for *following* Jesus? Because the blessings that come from following *Jesus* far outweigh any cost we may incur.

What are some of the blessings we receive from following Him?

Philippians 4:12-13

_____

_____

Isaiah 41:10

_____

_____

Psalm 1:1-3

_____

_____

Psalm 23:1-4

_____

_____

2 Corinthians 9:8

_____

_____

Philippians 4:7

BACK ON DRY LAND

In addition to the blessings the above verses promise us, when we follow *Jesus*, we live our lives now and for all eternity in the presence of God. This is called *Coram Deo* (before God). While this may give you flashbacks of your mother telling you that *Jesus is always watching* as a way to get you to behave, that is not quite what it means. What *Coram Deo* does mean is that Christians live their lives in the presence of God, under the authority of God, and to the glory of God. It's understanding that everything we do, say, think, and believe is under the watchful eye of our Sovereign, Almighty Father. And while that may sound scary, it is actually incredibly encouraging and freeing because God, Who knows and sees every dark and dirty part of us, still loved us enough to send His only Son to die for us, so that we can be reconciled with Him and spend eternity with Him.

David understood and embraced *Coram Deo*. As he writes in **Psalm 139:1-16**:

> *O Lord, you have searched me and known me!*
> *You know when I sit down and when I rise up;*
> *you discern my thoughts from afar.*
> *You search out my path and my lying down*
> *and are acquainted with all my ways.*
> *Even before a word is on my tongue,*
> *behold, O Lord,you know it altogether.*
> *You hem me in, behind and before,*
> *and lay your hand upon me.*
> *Such knowledge is too wonderful for me;*
> *it is high; I cannot attain it.*
> *Where shall I go from your Spirit?*
> *Or where shall I flee from your presence?*
> *If I ascend to heaven, you are there!*
> *If I make my bed in Sheol, you are there!*
> *If I take the wings of the morning*
> *and dwell in the uttermost parts of the sea,*

> *even there your hand shall lead me,*
> *and your right hand shall hold me.*
> *If I say, "Surely the darkness shall cover me,*
> *and the light about me be night,"*
> *even the darkness is not dark to you;*
> *the night is bright as the day,*
> *for darkness is as light with you.*
> *For you formed my inward parts;*
> *you knitted me together in my mother's womb.*
> *I praise you, for I am fearfully and wonderfully made.*
> *Wonderful are your works;*
> *my soul knows it very well.*
> *My frame was not hidden from you,*
> *when I was being made in secret,*
> *intricately woven in the depths of the earth.*
> *Your eyes saw my unformed substance;*
> *in your book were written, every one of them,*
> *the days that were formed for me,*
> *when as yet there was none of them.*

We are not just the result of a sperm and an egg coming together. We were intentionally and carefully formed by the Almighty Creator! And God did not create us just to walk away after we were born and leave us to our own devices. He is with us every second of every day. God, Who began a good work in us, will see it to completion. *Coram Deo* is not God watching and waiting to pounce on every wrong thing we do; Jesus has already paid the price for all of that. *Coram Deo* is our understanding that God is completely sovereign over every aspect of our lives. It is our desire to want to obey and honor God in every area of our life—not because we fear punishment, but because we are so grateful for all that He has done for us! To live *Coram Deo* is to embrace that God sees every single facet of us and to desire all of it to be glorifying and pleasing to Him. To live *Coram Deo* is not to worry about the costs of *following* Jesus because the benefit of following *Jesus* far outweighs any cost we would ever have to pay.

SUMMARY

For millions of martyred men and women throughout history, including all but one of Jesus' apostles, the cost of *following* Jesus was death. It was a price they were willing to pay to follow *Him*. Would we be willing to pay the ultimate cost for *following* Jesus? None of us can probably answer that for sure, but knowing what may be asked of us and understanding the immense blessings we receive from following *Jesus* will give us the strength we need to face anything that may be asked of us!

Perhaps some of the martyrs called the following Scriptures to mind when facing persecution:

- **1 Corinthians 2:9** says, "'*What no eye has seen, nor ear heard, nor the heart of man imagined, what God has prepared for those who love him.*'"

- In **John 8:12**, Jesus said, "*I am the light of the world. Whoever follows me will not walk in darkness, but will have the light of life.*'"

What has God prepared for those who love Him? What is the light of life? In the next chapter, we will answer these questions.

NOTES

_____

_____

_____

_____

_____

_____

_____

_____

_____

_____

_____

_____

_____

_____

_____

_____

_____

_____

NO HALF-TRUTHS ALLOWED

GETTING YOUR TOES WET

Are you a Christian? If you answered yes, why do you say that you are?

_____

_____

_____

Do you believe that all religions are equally valid or that "all paths lead to Heaven"?

_____

_____

_____

Do you think that as long as someone "believes in God," they are saved?

_____

_____

_____

Why is it so important that we get all of this right? Because of what Jesus came to save us from: God's wrath. Therefore, a false or half-truth Gospel message is not what you want to be believing yourself or sharing with others.

We're not trying to step on any toes here, although we may. What we are trying to do is to make you examine for yourself about what you believe and what you are sharing with others. Christians are to examine and test themselves. They should literally consider the question, "Am I really a Christian?" Paul tells the Corinthian church to do just that in **2 Corinthians 13:5**: *"Examine yourselves, to see whether you are in the faith. Test yourselves. Or do you not realize this about yourselves, that Jesus Christ is in you?—unless indeed you fail to meet the test!"*

DIVING IN DEEP

Jesus, the One and Only Way

In the closing verses of John 9, we see Jesus talking to the Pharisees who are questioning Him after He healed the man who was born blind. This leads us into John 10, which is really a continuation of the conversation. In John 10:1-10, Jesus is talking to them about a sheep pen, the shepherd of the sheep, the Great Shepherd, and the door to the pen. The Church are the sheep; and they are exposed to deceivers, false prophets, and false teachers, who come to steal, kill, and destroy. These imposters are the ones who climb over the wall to get into the sheep pen. They are not true shepherds; they are not true pastors. The true shepherds are those pastors who have received a true calling from God (which Jesus is telling the Pharisees they did not receive).

As for true shepherds, Jesus is also showing Himself as THE true Shepherd. But more importantly for this lesson, Jesus is also explaining here that He is <u>the Gate</u>. Jesus is the only true Way into the pen with the rest of the fold.

Read the following Scriptures, and write down what they say about salvation:

Acts 10:42-43

_____

_____

Matthew 1:21

_____

_____

John 3:36

_____

_____

1 Timothy 2:5-6

_____

_____

1 John 5:11-12

_____

_____

Revelation 7:10, 20:15

_____

_____

Jesus tells us that He is the Good Shepherd, and He warns us about the "hired hands." *Read **John 10:11-18**. Then write down what the following verses say about the unrighteous shepherds of God's people:*

Ezekiel 34:2-6

_____

_____

Zechariah 11:16-17

_____

_____

The hired hands are neglectful and do not care for the flock. Today, they are neglectful pastors who do not teach the sheep the deep theological and doctrinal truths of Scripture. They leave the flock with a shallow knowledge of God and His Word. They also leave the sheep and run away when the wolves come—wolves who offer false teaching and promote heresies within the flock. Often, these neglectful "hired hands" will neglect their own study and learning. God has standards for those shepherding His sheep.

Read the following passages, and write down what God requires of someone being an overseer of His sheep:

1 Timothy 3:1-7

_____

_____

Titus 1:4-11

_____

_____

1 Peter 5:1-3

_____

_____

Wolves in Sheep's Clothing and an Anti-Deception Self-Examination

The Sermon on the Mount is one of the most well-known teachings to a Christian. It is Jesus' sermon to those who are already professing Christians, telling them what Kingdom life should look like now. This is how it will eventually be in the new heavens and earth. Toward the end of the sermon, He talks about the wide gate and the narrow gate. Since He's talking to professing Christians here, we know that He is giving a warning that there are those who profess to be His sheep, but who are actually on the wide path.

Read **Matthew 7:13-16** and answer the following:

What gate do we need to enter by? What is the wide gate like? Where does the wide gate lead (v. 13)?

_____

_____

What is the narrow gate like? Where does it lead (v. 14)?

_____

_____

What are Christians to beware of? What will they look like? What are they really (v. 15)?

_____

_____

How can you recognize them (v. 16)?

_____

_____

Jesus is warning Christians in this passage about false teachers and warning them that the gate is narrow. There are many people who believe they are Christians, but they've been fed a false gospel—one that is centered on them, their hopes, and their dreams, with promises that God will fulfill them all. The warning about the gate being narrow—as well as Jesus' warnings from the book of John about false teachers, pastors, and false shepherds—should make you examine yourself and what kind of teaching you are believing. In the parable of the ten virgins, we see the results of someone believing they are ready for the King to return, but in the end, finding out that they aren't.

Read **Matthew 7:21-23** and **Matthew 25:1-13** and answer the following questions:

What is the gist of Matthew 7:21-23?

_____

_____

In what ways did the ten virgins seem to be the same?

_____

_____

_____

What are the differences between the two groups of virgins?

_____

_____

_____

When they first left, how many of them thought they were well-prepared and that they had what they needed?

_____

_____

The ten virgins all looked alike from the outside. They all looked like they were prepared. But they weren't. It is very possible to think you are a Christian—to do a lot of good works, serve in the church, and do all of the things one thinks a Christian should do—only to find out at the end of your life that you are not one! False teachers are nothing new. They lead people down wide paths of "easy Christianity" every day. You're probably sitting under a false shepherd or false teacher if you're hearing that God wants you to succeed, be happy, be rich, etc.; if the majority of your teaching comes from people who are focused on encouraging, supporting, and affirming you without often rebuking you; if your Christianity is based on God fulfilling your plans and your purposes; or if it's focused on what you can get from God and not on the glory and majesty of Christ and what He has done for you!

Ask yourself the following questions about the teaching you are getting from most sources:

Do I feel convicted of my sin against God when I'm being taught?

_____

_____

Is the teaching I'm getting mostly focused on making my life better, or is it focusing on Christ and what He did for me?

_____

_____

Am I being told God has a wonderful plan for me to succeed if I make the right choices, or am I being taught that God is Sovereign and working through both the good and bad things in my life because He is sovereignly and providentially in control of all of it?

Do I get taught chunks of Scripture that get explained, so that it helps me understand the Bible?

The warnings about false teaching are in the Bible for a purpose. False prophets were popular with the people of the day in Bible times because they told people what their "itching ears" wanted to hear. The true prophets were often hated for their message. They had the true words from God—often words of coming judgment. However, they also carried God's messages of coming hope!

Are you relying on a gospel that makes you feel good? One that lets you live how you want without any conviction at all? One that tells you your problems are the result of something (or someone) else, other than your own sin, or maybe blaming Satan for everything "bad"? Are you relying on a gospel that sounds like "the world's" humanistic, self-help psychology? Are you being told that the Gospel is about helping other people in tangible ways, and by doing so, you're helping yourself? Is the gospel you're relying on based on your moral character and how well you're keeping the standard?

Ask yourself the following questions:

Do I consider myself a Christian because I go to church, serve others, and am generally a good person?

Do I desire to be a Christian because I've been taught it is the way to achieve blessings in this life?

Am I willing to accept that the Christian life is not necessarily going to be one of blessing upon blessing and being a strong "warrior" for God; but rather, it is a life of realizing more and more that I'm more wretched than I ever thought I was, but more loved than I ever hoped to be?

Am I relying on anything else, other than Jesus' substitutionary death on the cross in my place, as the only way to not be an enemy of God any longer?

_____

_____

BACK ON DRY LAND

What we are taught about salvation is what we will rely on for salvation. What we are taught about God or not taught about God will affect our thoughts, our emotions, our expectations in this life, how we interact with the world, and everything else! How well we know and understand the Bible, both the Old Testament and the New Testament, and how well we understand its theological and doctrinal truths will affect every aspect of our lives. The Bible is God's Word to us. It was written so that God's people could understand it. The only way to protect yourself against false teachers is to know the Bible for yourself.

There are a lot of false gospels out there today. Some are completely devoid of the truth. Others are half-truths, not the complete Gospel message. We'll say it again—what we're taught about salvation is what we will rely on for salvation. And along with that, what we're relying on for salvation is what we'll teach others about salvation. To end this lesson, we'll take a brief look at some things being taught today that are NOT the Gospel. These are spelled out more fully in the book *No Half-Truths Allowed: Understanding the Complete Gospel Message*.

HALF-TRUTHS BEING TAUGHT TODAY
(What is NOT the Gospel?)

Declaring that "Jesus is Lord" alone is not the Gospel. Jesus is both Lord and Messiah. If you claim He is Lord of your life, you will want to make sure He is your Savior first.

"Just ask Jesus into your heart" is not the Gospel. Did you know that this phrase is not anywhere in the Bible? It's confusing; it tells the person absolutely nothing they need to know to be saved; and it's been called "the greatest heresy in the American, Evangelical, and Protestant church."[5]

Getting people to say the "sinner's prayer" is not the Gospel. Church services and altar calls focused on getting people to move forward and "make a commitment" are often lacking in telling them they are sinners and enemies of God. They have no idea why or even that they need a Savior.

---

5   Paul Washer, "Shocking Youth message," Accessed October 18, 2018, http://www.heartcrymissionary.com/sermons-en#!sid=1.

Your testimony is not the Gospel. Testimonies are wonderful ways to share what God has done in your life, but they are your experiences; and you can't save people with your story alone. The Gospel message is what people need to hear to respond and be saved.

Doing deeds of mercy and justice are not the same as spreading the Gospel. You have to actually use words to tell them the Gospel message.

Transforming the culture into a moralistic society is not the Gospel. Legislating God-honoring laws is a good thing to do, and the Religious Right of the 1970s had some good things in mind with regard to having a more moral society; but legislation doesn't produce heart change, and morals never save anyone.

Partnering with God to bring the Kingdom to Earth is not the Gospel. Helping the poor in tangible ways is important, and helping people should be an outworking of the Christian life; but no matter how much good work we do on Earth, it is not the same as sharing the Gospel, and it will not bring the Kingdom here. God does not need us as a partner to do anything!

SUMMARY

The Church is the Bride of Christ. And those of us who consider ourselves part of it need to ask ourselves some hard questions, starting with "Am I really a Christian?" If so, "What exactly do I believe and why?"

As God's chosen people, we need to make sure we are doing what we were created to do—glorify Him and enjoy Him forever! To do that, we need to know His Word, and we need to follow it. We need to spread the Gospel message, and we need to do it correctly! Will it be easy? Sometimes. Will it be hard? Sometimes. But it needs to be done. Therefore, let's make it our aim to glorify God by taking the message of the cross and making it central to everything else. *"For the word of the cross is folly to those who are perishing, but to us who are being saved it is the power of God* (1 Cor. 1:18).

NOTES

_____

_____

_____

_____

_____

_____

BIBLIOGRAPHY

Merriam-Webster. *s.v.* "Incarnation." https://www.merriam-webster.com/dictionary/incarnation (accessed 03/01/2019).

The New Strong's Exhaustive Concordance. Nashville, TN: Thomas Nelson Publishers, 1990.

Pence, Michael. "Remarks by Vice President Pence at Ministerial To Advance Religious Freedom." Speech, The White House, July 26, 2018. https://www.whitehouse.gov/briefings-statements/remarks-vice-president-pence-ministerial-advance-religious-freedom/.

Washer, Paul. "Shocking Youth Message." Sermon. July 27, 2002. Accessed October 18, 2018. http://www.heartcrymissionary.com/sermons-en#!sid=1.

ABOUT THE AUTHORS

ROSE SPILLER

CHRISTINE PAXSON

Rose and her husband, Ed, have been married over thirty-three years. They have four children who are spread out in Pennsylvania, Georgia, and Mississippi. They recently sold their home in Lancaster County, PA, to live full-time in their RV so they can divide their time between their four children and eight grandchildren. Rose enjoys all types of crafting, but especially quilting and crocheting, cooking, and reading.

Chris and her husband, John, have been married over thirty years, and they currently reside in Lancaster County, PA, with their many cats! They have twin boys who serve in the United States Air Force. Chris enjoys travelling, especially to visit her boys, golfing, reading, and entertaining.

Chris and Rose have been teaching Bible Studies for over twenty years. They have written several expository Bible Studies including ones on the Book of Daniel, the Book of Judges, the Book of Genesis, Women in Scripture, and the Sermon on the Mount.

They are co-founders of Proverbs 9:10 Ministries—a ministry focused on bringing women to a deeper understanding of God's Word. They co-host the podcast *No Trash, Just Truth!*, available on all podcast platforms. They also speak at women's conferences and retreats.

Both Chris and Rose have completed the "Dimensions of Faith" Program at Gordon-Conwell Theological Seminary and are currently enrolled in the "Institute" Program from BiblicalTraining.Org and take courses from Reformed Theological Seminary.

Look for their second book, *The Bible in Six*, an overview of all sixty-six books of the Bible, due out next winter!

PROVERBS 9:10
MINISTRIES

For more information about
Christine Paxson and Rose Spiller
and
No Half-Truths Allowed Study Guide
please connect at:

www.proverbs910ministries.com
www.facebook.com/prov910
proverbs910ministries@gmail.com
@prov_910

For more information about
AMBASSADOR INTERNATIONAL
please connect at:

www.ambassador-international.com
@AmbassadorIntl
www.facebook.com/AmbassadorIntl

If you enjoyed this book, please consider leaving us a review on Amazon, Goodreads, or our website.

Also check out Chris and Rose's Podcast No Trash, Just Truth! *Streaming now on all platforms.*

More from Ambassador International

In today's world of instant communication, any problems with cellular service or Wi-Fi access can be a major disruption to one's day. But there is one kind of communication that is always reliable and never disrupts: prayer.

Prayer: The Most Reliable Wireless Communication
by Rev. John Clark Mayden, Jr.

Everyone has baggage!

We all have something that keeps us from living fully for the Lord, but Christ wants us to give our baggage to Him so we can follow Him freely. In *Pack Your Baggage, Honey, We're Moving to Paris!* Anne Farnum explores the different kinds of baggage we carry. She also focuses on the baggage that King Saul hid behind and compares it to that which David left behind to run toward the giant.

Pack Your Baggage, Honey, We're Moving to Paris!
by Anne Farnum

With kindness, honesty, and Biblical truth, author Christen Price encourages readers to overcome the hurdles of perfection by finding balance instead of breaking down, receiving others in love by releasing all anxieties to God and rejoicing in the moments worth celebrating, and discovering that the antidote to perfection is embracing the beauty of imperfection and presenting not only yourself, but your home, in an artful way so you can give and receive joy.

Invited: Live a Life of Connection, Not Perfection
by Christen Price

CPSIA information can be obtained
at www.ICGtesting.com
Printed in the USA
LVHW100217210121
677080LV00011B/262